PHILOSOPHICAL FOOTBALL

Philosophical Football

The Team that Plays with Strength in Depth

Mark Perryman

MAINSTREAM
PUBLISHING

EDINBURGH AND LONDON

published in association with

PHILOSOPHY FOOTBALL
Sporting outfitters of intellectual distinction

First published in Great Britain in 1999 by
MAINSTREAM PUBLISHING COMPANY (EDINBURGH) LTD
7 Albany Street
Edinburgh EH1 3UG

ISBN 1 84018 209 1

A catalogue record for this book is available from the British Library

Typeset in Times New Roman
Printed and bound in Finland by WSOY

Contents

The Magic Sponge and Other Helpful Gestures

Philosophy Football was born just in time for Christmas 1994 and sorted out more than a few last-minute stocking-filler problems. Five years later and we mail out to more than 20,000 avid fellow-philosophers keen to add the latest great mind's words of wisdom on the people's game to their kit list. Each of the shirts from the self-styled 'sporting outfitters of intellectual distinction', you see, features a few words to the wise emblazoned across chest or breast (delete as applicable) with name and squad number on the back. Sounds simple enough, but what other team – apart from *Philosophy Football* – would feature Camus in goal, Blanchflower at the heart of the defence, Oscar Wilde in midfield and the god-like genius of Pelé up front?

Hugh Tisdale has started describing himself as the 'eyes' of *Philosophy Football*. What he means is that I'm the 'mouth', the gobby one who puts himself about a bit, media-wise, while Hugh comes up with the superlative designs that make for our sartorial excellence. Add his concern for tidy systems and attention to detail instead of a desk overwhelmed by piles of sprawling papers that I prefer and this is a partnership of promise. Notwithstanding the fact that Spurs, my side, have at last started to get the odd result against Aston Villa, Hugh's lot, we really do get on famously.

Pedro Santos and his Fifth Column crew occupy a weird space sort of on top of Kentish Town tube station in North London. They print our shirts to the highest-possible standard, and have been waiting an inordinately long time for the proverbial cheque in the post. Without Pedro's patience I would have been down the dole office long ago.

Philosophical Football is the cerebral spin-off from all this frantic fashion-business stuff: my bid not just for some academic credibility but also to crack the sort of jokes White Hart Lane's queue for the bagels could do with. Having crafted the 100 per cent cotton versions to perfection, now's my chance to dream up how this mob would have actually played the game. Without the following people though, my warped imagination would have hardly got going: Pat Coyne and his Collected Works of Marx and Engels CD-ROM thingumybob confounded my know-how of cyberspace but helped me a lot with the Marx chapter; Adrian Smith from the Edward Boyle Library at Leeds University dished the lesser-known footballing background on Shostakovich to me in a sealed brown envelope; and Simon Welch wrenched himself away from the travails of Crewe Alexandra's league form to tell me more about Kierkegaard than it's probably healthy to know. Assorted kind fellows waxed lyrically about George Orwell's hatred of football; Stefan Howald and Adam Morton were particularly persistent with their insights, and David Clifford gave me chapter and verse on Machiavelli, in English and the original Italian to boot. Hugh Tisdale tracked down the original source of Paul Cézanne's sad letter to his mate confessing that the long wait for a goal might yet be forlorn – a fear most of us have shared at some time in our football-supporting careers. Danny Sperling proved himself a dab hand at ancient Greek to sort out Homer. Leon Culbertson at Brighton University's bizarrely named 'Chelsea School' – I wonder if they have their lectures in a shed – convinced me that Jean-Paul Sartre really did write about football in his *Critique of Dialectical Reason*. And finally Richard Skellington, editor of the Open University's *Society Matters* newsletter unearthed Jacques Derrida's work on the ball that's out of play. So if you don't believe my wilful misrepresentation of the facts, blame these people, not me.

As a student of Philosophical Football I'm constantly on the look out for new geniuses to add to the team. The deal is, provide a quote, authenticate it and if we consider it worthy of T-shirted immortality then the first one off the production line is yours. Some of those I'm peculiarly keen to recruit are Foucault, Trotsky, Andy Warhol, Pythagoras, Malcom X,

Proudhon, Luxemburg, Kollantai and Rabbie Burns. Send in any quotes and source details to me at *Philosophy Football*, PO Box 10684, London N15 6XA, England.

Finding out whether this hopefully mighty tome stands up to at least a cursory glance of academic scrutiny while providing a rib-tickler of a read is no mean feat, so I am indebted to the combined talents of Wendy Wheeler, Tim Bewes, Geoff Andrews, Jeremy Gilbert and Mel Barker. The fact that you grinned or smiled and didn't slam me too often for my theoretical clangers did wonders for my confidence and endurance.

The ideological underpinning of all this has once again been provided by Stephen Parrott and his frankly unique 'Football, Culture and Society' evening classes at London's Birkbeck College. They run every May and June, and there's no better way to pep up your end-of-season blues and do wonders for your after-match analysis.

Bill Campbell at Mainstream was kind enough to take this book on. He entertained me at London's infamous Groucho Club, a sure-fire way to convince most authors they're important. Thankfully, in this case, Bill followed it up with an enthusiasm and flair that cannot be faulted. It's almost enough to make an Englishman cheer Bill's native Scotland on – almost, but not quite. And thanks to Camilla James and Andrea Fraile, who corrected my misspellings and misunderstandings of the history of civilisation along with the odd mistaken footballing reference thrown in too, just to catch them unawares.

I can only be held responsible for the words in *Philosophical Football*. So a big shout to Tim Bradford of *When Saturday Comes* for bringing the text to life with his inspired cartoons and to Sarah Edwards for tracking down more philosophers' portraits than she'd probably care to remember.

Spurs, we are talking the first half of 1999 here, supplied more than the occasional moment of footballing hope, a very welcome bit of silverware and at Old Trafford on Sunday, 17 May, occasioned the most surreal chant I've heard yet at a ground: '1–0 And We're Trying to Lose'. Oh, that Freud were there to analyse this crisis of inferior expectations, but that will have to wait for my next book.

Finally, Anne Coddington has put up with me, my mess and a next-door seat in the Spurs' West Stand for more seasons than I'm sure anyone else would bother enduring. It must be something in the water. I promised her I'd make a million, but have this unerring desire to change the world instead. All I can say is that sitting beside Anne at the Lane is the most exciting thing I can imagine, notwithstanding the odd goal from Ginola, and Anderton passing his medical. For all that, and much more, this book wouldn't have been possible without Anne's love and inspiration.

A Word from the Dugout

Having already made my first-team selection of the good, the bad and almost certainly not David Mellor for my first book *Philosophy Football: Eleven Great Thinkers Play it Deep*, I thought it would be nigh-on impossible to find a second squad to match that lot. After all, *Philosophy Football* included Albert Camus in goal, William Shakespeare as a playmaker, Sun Tzu lording it over them as a midfield general and Umberto Eco signing on as centre-forward.

But with God, Marx, Homer and Sartre, who's to say the eleven making their long-awaited debut for *Philosophical Football: The Team that Plays with Strength in Depth* wouldn't have the licking of this earlier lot? God alone has all the powers that any one team could wish for from a man behind the sticks. I selected a quote from the Old Testament to illustrate just how much the Bible can tell us about a game of two halves but with Jesus on the end of a cross, Peter denying him three times and the disciples, minus their own Judas, pretty adept at picking balls out of nets who's to say there aren't more where these wise words came from?

The idea behind this book is delightfully simple. Take eleven of the world's greatest minds then imagine how they would have turned out if their brains had been in their boots instead of their heads. Learned philosophers have used the characters of *Winnie the Pooh* to explain the inner logic of positivism, not to mention the global appeal of all things to do with Tao, so why not football? And when apparently otherwise sensible members of the adult population believe the way they arrange their furniture could affect their chances of wealth, happiness and a long life courtsey of Feng Shui, eleven individuals in ill-fitting shorts chasing a spherical object across a park seems an eminently reasonable way of visualising the organisation of society.

Germaine Greer earns her position for her championing of 'the idiot savant' at the heart of England's national team. As England tumbled their way out of Euro '96 – thanks to yet another manager who reckoned practising taking penalties was beneath his supposedly prodigiously gifted squad – Germaine waxed lyrical in *The Independent*: 'I was astonished by the strange nobility of the spectacle. England was a team as few national sides have ever been; they threw themselves at the Germans. The instinct for self-preservation was in abeyance, overridden by something more basic and utterly mysterious.' It's hard to believe England actually lost. Germaine, like any self-respecting fan, lost herself in helpless romanticism.

Beside Germaine and her unsung career as a football commentator, the likes of Marx, Kierkegaard and Homer may seem stranger choices. But have a look at all those Olympic scenes adorning those Greek urns; isn't there the merest hint of football as one of the original Olympian sports? Surely, yes. And as for Marx, with his mate Friedrich Engels examining the condition of the working class between the showers of rain that hang over Manchester, surely Fred would have reported to Karl of dirty-faced street urchins knocking a ball about in the streets. This is the home of the red army, after all. Could this not have been the inspiration of the greatest ideas to cast a spectre over Europe this century? Apart, of course, from Fergie's unbridled desire to lift the European Cup. Kierkegaard is Danish, and they love their football. So is it so fanciful to think of Søren sneaking down to FC Copenhagen between agonising over the complexities of individual choice? Well, maybe it is, I'll leave that to you to decide. But as Søren's fellow-countryman, Jostein Gaarder, has managed to flog the odd few hundred-thousand copies of his own translation of philosophy into words of less than two syllables, *Sophie's World*, I'm hoping for a bit of a result.

Not all my players are as divorced from the game as Paul Cézanne and Jean-Paul Sartre might appear to be at first glance. Jacques Derrida confessed to one interviewer, 'We played until it was dark. I dreamt of becoming a professional footballer.' The mind must boggle at what turned this clearly level-headed adolescent from football to the wilder shores of postmodern theorising. What a loss. One can imagine the shout going going up now, 'Ooh-Aah Jacques Derridaaaaah'. And as for Dmitri Shostakovich, he not only composed an opus entitled 'Football' but also provided the music for a ballet, *The Golden Age*. Nothing unusual about that you might think, but, hold on a minute, this was a performance built around a plot that traces the conflict between fascists and a Soviet football team touring the West. The piece reaches its climax with a dance of footballers and the proletariat, united in their celebration of work. Dmitri was revealed by his biographer as 'A great football fan, he often came down to Moscow specially for a match. He would send Ronya a telegram the day before to ask him to reserve tickets', Shostakovich, like so many others like him, had this secret life of football that has lain hidden by the dusts of time. *Philosophical Football* is their chance to be imagined if things had just worked out differently for them.

By the time George Orwell turned his hand to commentating on the Moscow Dynamo 1945 British tour he was already all bitter and twisted about most things Soviet. Orwell was a brilliant exposer of the immoral cant that passes for politics once politicians, left or right, have their hands on power, but we can still baulk at his overblown

15

claim: 'There are quite enough real causes of trouble already, and we need not add to them by encouraging young men to kick each other on the shins amid the roars of infuriated spectators.' United by the love of football, the game at an international level always has the potential to point to what we, as fans, have in common as much as what divides us: the will to win, or at least not to get home before the postcards arrive.

As for Machiavelli, if there's one philosopher who hints at the parallel universe that players and managers occupy alongside these seminal thinkers, Old Nick does. A dive in the penalty area or the barked instructions from the dugout to hack down the other lot's number nine, 'Machiavellian' was made for describing the seamier side of football, and so Old Nick's selection is justifiable – even if it is hard to prove he ever kicked a ball in anger, or joy coming to think of it.

Philosophy Football, the company from whose T-shirts the idea of this book sprang, has been described variously by the *Sunday Times* as 'the sun-dried tomatoes of the football-shirt business' and by *Graphis*, the international style bible for graphic designers, as 'seeking to fuse the musings of the world's greatest philosophers with the beautiful game'. Sun-dried and fusing, but not too heavy, I hope. For as Karl, Germaine and Jean-Paul would surely agree, at the end of the day, football's a funny old game. So just go out there across the next hundred-plus very odd pages or so, and enjoy yourself. You can't ask any more of an author and his readers than that, can you?

Mark Perryman

Meet the Team

1. God (OBC-)

The word of God as written in the Bible has been a worldwide bestseller for generations and is likely to remain so until Armageddon. An eternal pot-boiler, the Bible features characters that have gone on to become household names including Joseph and Jesus, who made it big in musicals too.

2. Germaine Greer (1938-)

One of the founders of modern feminism, Germaine Greer wrote a key text of '70s women's liberation, *The Female Eunuch*. An early champion of the sexual revolution, her most recent book, *The Whole Woman*, revisits her original ideals to demand not just equality for women, but something better.

3. Karl Marx (1818-83)

'Workers of the world unite, you have nothing to lose but your chains' is probably one of the most famous phrases of all time. Throw in 'the philosophers have only interpreted the world, the point is to change it', and you have a measure of Karl Marx's historical significance. Love him or loathe him, nobody can afford to ignore his work.

4. Dmitri Shostakovich (1906-75)

Commonly regarded as one of the finest composers of the twentieth century, Shostakovich's music appealed to both modernists and traditionalists. He spent his entire life working under the regime that ruled the Soviet Union, falling in and out of favour with Stalin and others with bewildering frequency.

5. Søren Kierkegaard (1813-55)

A hugely influential thinker of the nineteenth century, Søren Kierkegaard wrote in emphatic opposition to the prevailing ideas of his time. Concerned principally with the significance of individual choice to the human condition, his legacy is most obvious in the body of thought known in the twentieth century as existentialism.

6. George Orwell (1903-50)

With *Animal Farm* and *Nineteen Eighty-Four*, George Orwell provided an inspired account of the awful consequences of totalitarian rule, even when it was supposedly 'in the name of the people'. Whether writing of war, empire or poverty Orwell brought his subjects, fictional or non-fictional, to life, and the politics he felt so strongly were never very far away either.

7. Niccolò Machiavelli (1469-1527)

A native of Florence, Machiavelli's writings on statecraft, most famously *The Prince*, gave birth to the prefix 'Machiavellian' that is used to describe a politics that sacrifices the means for the sake of the ends. No other writer so epitomises the murky world of diplomacy and the unerring desire to survive that sums up what it is to be a politician today.

8. Paul Cézanne (1839-1906)

One of the most important of the Post-Impressionist painters, Paul Cézanne produced works that were rarely anything less than radical in conception. He combined realism with a bold and imaginative use of colours while breaking up his landscapes and portraits into geometrical shapes that pointed to his eventual influence upon the Cubists.

9. Homer (c.750-c.700BC)

Standing at the very beginning of Greek literature, nobody can be quite sure of precisely when Homer lived. What is certain is that his epic works, the *Iliad* and the *Odyssey,* have had an incalculable influence on Western philosophy's varied explanations of the meaning of life ever since they were first written in those faraway mists of time.

10. Jean-Paul Sartre (1905-80)

Jean-Paul Sartre was a member of the French underground during the Second World War. Novelist and playwright, he was a major influence on European post-war intellectual life. Jean-Paul came up with the term 'existentialism' and in his later life embraced his own particular version of Marxism whilst never losing sight of the centrality of such concepts as consciousness, freedom and absurdity.

11. Jacques Derrida (1930-)

Jacques Derrida is one of the most important figures in contemporary philosophy. Yet he is one the discipline's greatest foes, undermining traditions and rules, questioning certainties, drawing on concepts from well beyond what has until now been defined as philosophy's accepted field. Deconstructing and destabilising is Derrida's strategy, making for a thinker who is difficult, but all the same necessary, to follow.

God

Southampton and Israel
Number 1 : Goalkeeper

'Am I my brother's keeper?'

The Bible, Genesis 3:9

A past master at making something out of nothing, there are some who say that God started his playing career with a big bang. It's certainly true that for five days he toiled away to good effect and when Saturday came he put in such a great performance that he had the whole world in his hands. No wonder he put his feet up on Sunday.

He was an early pioneer of floodlit football – if light was needed then let there be light was God's attitude. This might not have been such a good idea, though, as he didn't believe in playing strips: bared to the elements was how he expected his first team-mates Adam and Eve to play. And when they broke God's strict diet regulations by snaffling up an apple on the sly, he punished them with a fig-leaf kit that was really rough on the skin, with all those roots and bits of earth getting caught up with what were, by now, naughty bits.

Adam and Eve were to blame also for the introduction of referees, red cards, linesmen and the like. Forbidden fruit, spare ribs, these two played havoc with their calorie counters, not to mention the way they snaked down the wing when you weren't looking. It wasn't long before God reckoned they were probably more trouble than they were worth. The rest of his first squad weren't much good either, he couldn't find eleven decent enough players to put a side out so he just thought sod 'em, and that Gomorrah wasn't much better either.

He needed players who could hunt out the ball then gather it up for the midfield. Cain and Abel showed some early promise at this, but Cain seemed in some doubt about whether he'd be better off in goal. His brother's keeper? No chance. Before you know it that Cain will be stabbing the lads in the back, thought God. And, when the towering presence of Babel in the middle of defence came crashing down to earth, God knew it was time to start all over again.

Getting his side to play to some kind of system was one possible answer. Noah gave the team a shape with his two-two-two-two-two formation. A winning streak began that lasted an amazing forty days and forty nights. Noah was a dab hand at soaking up the pressure as his penalty area became flooded with awkward balls. And then, however bad it got at the back, Noah was no wet blanket. Soon enough God needed a book of numbers to keep a note of his players as his squad started to grow. Abraham joined the team, full of early promise, but he had his barren periods, too. For a time it looked like Abraham might have to sacrifice his son, Isaac, if he was to keep his place in God's side, but God relented, keeping faith with them both and signing them up for another season or two. As time went on, God built the team around the pairing of Jacob – who could climb above most centre-forwards with his famous ladder – and Joseph – who persuaded the club to invest in a strip of many colours that was a cut above the loin cloths they had been wearing. Joseph, in fact, was a bit of an all-round dreamer taken to flights of fancy like imagining Arsenal were a flair team and Everton still one of the big five. But when he was transferred to Egypt he had to face up to the harsh reality of working his way up through the pyramid system. So God gave him his due. Joseph had worked hard and his dream of seven good years at the top, with titles and cups to show for it, did come true. And when the seven lean years came, as they always do, Joseph managed to get through the goal drought his side was suffering from.

If Joseph's side was to survive, heading rapidly back towards the bottom of the pyramid, he knew he'd need the odd reserve in hand. And so he introduced the idea of a substitute, no longer just the eleven players, but a playing staff of twelve – though the rivalries between them meant things had a tendency to turn a bit tribal.

When Joseph's time was up, God – who has an uncanny knack of being there when you most need him – picked Moses as his replacement. Under Moses, God's side would no longer be lambs to the slaughter, he would part defences and the exodus of quality players back to their original homeland, Israel, could begin. Moses was a bit of a disciplinarian, issuing commandments like they were written in stone. He had no time for those who worshipped false idols. For every Eric Cantona there was a Teddy Sherringham, as the lost tribe of Mancunians spread far and wide would surely one day find out. But his most precious rule of thumb was for managers, not players: 'Do not covet thy neighbour's donkey.' Signing Carlton Palmer wasn't going to be the answer to anyone's prayers.

Moses lasted longer than most of God's selections, but after forty years in the wilderness God reckoned it was about time to shake things up a bit. The team's fortunes started to change when they found a way to break down the defensive wall that had been Jericho FC's saving grace. Boy, did the lads blow their own trumpets after that first victory set them on the road to glory. From here on in, God wasn't going to put up with any rivals. With him looking over them, the players knew they could do just about anything, but if they ignored him then their defences would be down and they'd be leaving themselves open to attack. The choice was theirs' alone.

Samson came in to shore up the defence for a while. He looked finished, though, after a scissor-kick from Delilah cut him down to size, but he brought the house down with one final barnstormer of a performance as he took the pillars of the Philistines' attack out for good. A career ended shamefully early. A timely reminder that God gave a lot to the side, but he took away too; transfer dealings were two-way even in these ancient times.

Of course, a cup run was always the best remedy to life's little disappointments. David was the hero of the team's greatest ever feat of cup giant-killing. With David slinging the ball into their half, Goliath and his big city side didn't stand a chance. David was in top form and playing well above his station. Poor old Goliath caught the blistering shot right between the eyes and never fully recovered. After the ignominy of being turfed out of the cup, he left to play out his days in the Asia Minor leagues.

Together the forward-line trio of David, Saul and Solomon went on to create Israel United, though David let the others down by harking on about City too. In fact Solomon wasn't much better either, appalling the parents of his youthful squad when he tried to cut his playing staff in half. Only kidding, mind, and he did go on to mine their rich seam of talent for many seasons to come. If they ever let him down, he promised them wage packets of sin rather than shekels. This was an option that strangely enough some seemed to prefer, until they discovered that the kit they'd have to play in was the itchiest yet: sackcloth with an ashes multiweave sewn in for bad measure.

All the same, Israel United were definitely God's dream team. This is what he'd worked so long and hard to achieve.

The spirit of the side was epitomised by the new talent they unearthed in young Daniel. Even when he could see the writing on the wall, with an unheard-of relegation battle beckoning, he was strong enough to be thrown into the Millwall Lion's Den and come out with a victory. The early promise that God had seen in the side seemed, at last, to be coming good. And when dyslexic prophets of the Baal tried their own way to Goaal, it was left to God's veteran captain, Elijah, to call down the shots from where they'd headed heavenwards into the upper tier and end Israel's goal drought himself. False profits were no way to run a club.

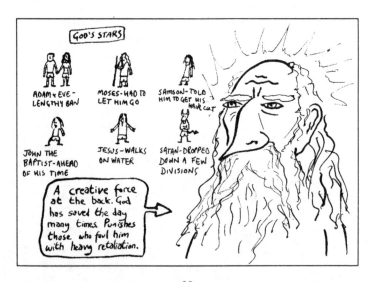

The best days, though, were yet to come. God knew he needed a man to sit at his right hand if he was to build a side that would last for eternity. And who better to entrust that awesome responsibility to than his own son, Jesus. Brought up to perform do-it-yourself miracles by his carpenter dad, Joseph, and the clean-living Mary, Jesus was watched from almost as soon as he could walk by those who would shepherd the flocks of talented youngsters through from the schoolboy ranks to their first-team debut. Three wise men from Leyton Orient were similarly convinced as soon as they clapped eyes on him that here was a star, one to follow all right.

Pretty soon Jesus paired up with his cousin, John, to make his first-team debut. God just wanted the two of them to put their playing toes in the water for starters, a ten-minute run-out towards the end of a game when his side were already 3–0 up would do nicely. But John wasn't having any of it. He wanted to get the two of them fully immersed in the game, a right proper baptism of fire, but no brimstone if you please. Sure enough, the two of them shone brightly, lighting up the game with their deft movement on and off the ball. Jesus made himself mighty popular after the game too – when he wasn't turning water into wine he was livening up the diet, after all they couldn't be expected to live off bread alone. The lads were well chuffed, but there was a sting in the tail (not that Jesus had one, of course). The chairman was making a mess of parking his camel into a tiny slot in the club oasis when Jesus helpfully pointed out that he'd no more fit his beast in there than get to heaven. That was the end of Jesus' all too brief honeymoon period at the club. It was time to break free and put his own side together, a move that had God's blessing.

Matthew, Mark, Luke and John were his back four, with Andrew and Peter fishing the ball out of the middle of the park to release James and Thomas on the wings. There were plenty who had their doubts about Thomas' ability to put the ball away, but Jesus reckoned that if he had the talent it would show in the end. Jesus was happy enough now; a squad of twelve who would do him proud and be ready to follow him to the ends of the earth. The lads did find his pre-match team talks a bit confusing, though. One moment it was all about about tough tackling, take the other lot's teeth and eyes out if they lay a hand or foot on us. The next, Jesus was imploring them not to get riled, put in a bit of mooning and turn those cheeks if it all got too much. And, as for retaliation, the lads would have to learn to forgive those who foul against them as they know not what they do. Temptation? It wasn't something the lads would be led into. Surely this would all add up to a right turning over? But it was a miracle, they were top of the table in next to no time. And 1–0 down at a difficult away game against Bethany FC, Lazarus helped them come back from the dead to turn the deficit into a 2–1 victory. Afterwards, the Bethany supporters started to turn nasty but

Jesus soon calmed them down with a challenge to start chucking stones only if they'd never stolen an ill-deserved victory themselves.

After Bethany away there was no looking back, though tragedy struck when cousin John lost his head as Salome danced through the defence and landed up with a goal on a plate. John never did make it back into the side. Still, most of the games went Jesus's way, his keeper just had to lay his hands on the ball and its back-of-the-net path was stopped. And as for running out of half-time pies, fat chance with Jesus taking over the club catering franchise from the evil empire of McDonald's. Five loaves and two fishes seemed strangely ample with home gates touching 5,000. From catering to the treatment room where the injured were expected to pick up their beds and get out on the training pitch, Jesus had it all sussed. When the heavens chucked it down, he simply changed the lads' studs – if he could walk on water then so could they. Prodigal sons came back after buying out their own contracts with teams they'd been sold to, and Jesus appointed a good Samaritan as his trainer to run on to treat any injuries. Jesus himself, though, preferred to apply what was soon enough dubbed the 'magic sponge'. Hamstring or tendon, achilles or shin-splints, Jesus seemed to have a ready answer to every affliction. He even washed the lads' feet after to keep verrucas, athlete's foot and the odd sinful spirit at bay.

The team began to think they were unbeatable. But when an agent came in with an offer of thirty pieces of silver to purchase Judas, things started to go all wrong. Judas ended up a right useless goal-hanger, betraying his early promise, but the damage had already been done. Peter too was finding his move from the rock of the midfield to between the posts difficult to cope with. He denied Jesus three times in an early-morning training session before the cock crowed but he was left full of self-doubt, his confidence shot to pieces. As for Jesus, he was being crucified by crosses that he kept ending up on the end of but unable to score the goals that the team so desperately needed. The new owners of the club asked the guv'nor, Pontius Pilate, for an answer and he promptly washed his hands of poor old Jesus. Of course he'd make a comeback, and just three days later he was already showing he could rise above the rest, but he was finished in this particular neck of the woods. The West Bank was no longer his, the North Bank never had been, so he was left to roam the earth, the eternal journeyman.

Robbed of their leader, the lads decided to plough on. One more-than-useful addition to the side proved to be Paul – he played a right blinder on one tricky away trip to Damascus and everyone was duly converted. He earned a bit of money on the side as a writer too, and his coverage of Corinthian Casuals' games was really something to write home about. Eventually he was transferred – like so many other players –

from the domestic league to Roma where he ended up playing under Nero. Nero was a notorious boss, on the fiddle while the stand burned. He would have gone down a storm at Doncaster Rovers in another life. It was a fairly miserable way to see out your career but it was still better than watching John Fashanu doing a passable impersonation of a Gladiator, so we can all be thankful for big mercies.

Jesus seemed to be well and truly off the scene now. But with God in the background the odd revelation was sure to brighten up the dullest of seasons, and there were plenty who still believed that Jesus's second coming couldn't be too far off. However the big fear remained that God's bitter rival, Satan, whom he thought he'd safely dispatched to the lower divisions, would make another bid to claw his way back to the top. With three number sixes to choose from and four thoroughbred wingers giving him plenty of width, Satan could be more than a match for just about anyone. But not God, he was having none of this. They thought it was all over but he was the beginning and the end of the greatest game ever played. Hand of God? There was plenty more where that came from, and if Satan scores God saves, for ever and ever.

Germaine Greer

Doncaster Belles and Australia
Number 2 : Right-back

'Football is an art more central to our culture than anything the Arts Council deigns to recognise.'

GERMAINE GREER, *The Independent*, 1996

Germaine Greer always plays with the one ball. But that doesn't mean she's content with just sweeping the ball up at the back, because she's also full of movement. The direct game is her approach to defensive duties, liberating space that seemed to have been denied her, then bewitching defenders with her occasionally silky skills. Attack is her best form of defence; she's out to win not simply settle for a draw, an equaliser is never enough. Coming out on top is what Germaine is all about.

Tough tackling and fast with it, Germaine is never going to be second to the ball. But if the rest of the defence can't keep up with her frantic play, she knows they'll leave themselves wide open to a backlash. Germaine relies on Susan Faludi to keep her eye open for such eventualities, though divisions of labour aren't normally Germaine's kind of thing. Faludi provides great cover at the back, as the long passes that might have caught Germaine unawares fly in, and marshals her second wave of defending midfielders to take all the pressure. But Germaine didn't only rely on the newcomer Faludi; veteran England international Mary Wolstonecraft was vindicating Germaine's faith in her old legs, refusing to give ground, home or away. Mary's talent had lain lost and undiscovered for too long, and Germaine was mighty proud to have resurrected her career. So it was with new and old stars at her side that Germaine set out to take her Belles on to greater things.

In the early days Marie Antoinette tried to persuade Germaine that she should let the players eat cake. She claimed all the carbohydrates and sugar would boost their stamina. Germaine wasn't convinced, but before she had time to make up her mind the hot-tempered Marie Antoinette had lost her head. Cut off in her prime, she was sacked from the side. Not the kind of woman Germaine would be able to build her team around, then.

Germaine knew that if her squad was to compete on an equal level with the big boys or, even better, win the odd trophy, she would have to sort out the team's positions. Tidying up at the back wasn't enough for Germaine, she wanted to lead from the front too. Funnily enough it was a bloke, John Stuart Mill, who was one of the first to raise this subject of where it was best for women like Germaine to play.

But John Stuart Mill was pretty much the exception. Germaine knew that for every one like him there would be a Tom, Dick or Harry to blow the whistle on her search for a side that would be their equal. Constance Markiewicz was one woman who looked like a winner, and never going to be happy with just a seat on the bench. The Pankhurst family too were hungry for goals, smashing to watch and with all the attributes Germaine knew her players would need to make the opposition really suffer. They had her vote, every time.

As Germaine's players began to emerge, Charles Darwin was one who doubted whether they'd ever have the physical strength to stop their eventual descent down the table. But another man, Friedrich Engels, disagreed. 'Look at the state of them,' Friedrich declared to all who would listen. He pointed to the origin of Germaine's team, confident that once she'd sorted out how to control the ball she would be ready to lead them to victory.

With Engels' support, Germaine introduced a handy pair of continentals to the squad. Clara Zetkin had the quality to bridge the division between the Belles and any men's sides they came up against, while, from faraway Russia, Alexandra Kollontai brought a collective approach to the defence – no more solo runs that could leave the Belles exposed at the back, but working together as a unit. Things started to look up as their home results began to go in Germaine's favour. But she still wasn't convinced that the club was the finished article yet, for as soon as her back was turned they would leak away goals. Relying on their home form wasn't going to get the Belles to the top, for domestic performances just weren't enough if you wanted to win the league.

Simone de Beauvoir showed Germaine the way her side could yet challenge for honours. Never coming off second best, Simone livened things up in the middle of the park. But it was Betty Friedan, a player of some mystique, who was to show that trapping the ball wasn't enough, the team needed to know what to do once they'd won possession. Playing at her best under floodlights, she put together a string of victories as she reclaimed the night for the Belles. Betty's success lay with persuading the team that fast, penetrating balls into the box weren't the be-all and end-all of the game. There was more than one way to score. Meanwhile, it might have been lonely out on the wing for Radclyffe Hall but she seemed to enjoy her game doing her own thing well enough. And as for Andrea Dworkin, she was more than capable of closing down opponents who offended her. Betty convinced the team that it was their bodies themselves who would win this game, with or without the supporters. And when Susan Brownmiller started to tighten things up at the back, Germaine knew they'd only lose against their will.

But the game doesn't always go the way you think it will. When they failed to get those equalisers, Germaine's team found themselves pushed wide, back into the margins. Simone de Beauvoir wasn't having any more of that though, she was determined that things would change for the better and she suggested to Germaine that the answer was to construct a whole new side. The colour purple, Alice Walker thought, would do for the kit. With their new tops, the Belles would knock the likes of Sigmund Freud unconscious as they began to practice a more confrontational game. Poor old Sigmund seemed to think it was all down to keeping the ball between his legs, but the Belles would rob the ball off him. There was no need to envy him once he'd lost it and they could go on their own sweet way. 'Robbed me blind,' Sigmund would complain.

'1–0 to the Belles!' Melanie Klein delighted in replying, the object now at her feet, not his.

Julia Kristeva was becoming hysterical, Freud and his mates were losing. They were giving up space to Germaine, and it didn't look as if the Belles would let the lead slip.

The Belles were on their way up the table and they'd leave somebody else to tidy up after them for a change. Camille Paglia wasn't the sort who gave the ball away easily, was she? Call her a victim and you'd get a right mouthful. Alongside her, Susan Sontag was playing deep. Though she did have this tendency to come over all metaphorical, with one eye on the game she gazed about her. But try to get past Susan and most men ended up making a right exhibition of themselves. The team were looking good, though nobody quite put it that way anymore for fear of misinterpretation, and the results were starting to go Germaine's way.

Still, the team were only human and sloppy defending could still lead to points dropped. Hannah Arendt found all of this a touch banal, she wasn't having any of this fancy Daniella pussyfooting around. To win, Hannah knew, would take a bit of evil in the box. Germaine agreed. They had a choice: clean up at the back, but end up losing the ball to somebody else who would enjoy the spoils of victory, or divorce themselves from these old ways. 'Never mind the language,' Dale Spender advised them, as Germaine was yellow-carded yet again for answering back to the referee. In Dale's book dissent was good for team spirit, and to win they'd have to fight long and hard, so attitude was all and never mind the suspensions.

The change was dramatic. 'Burnt their bridges', Germaine's critics pontificated. 'Burnt our bras!' she angrily corrected them, as the Belles' traditional supporters went up in flames. However those fifty–fifty balls still refused to go in Germaine's favour, and though she counselled against the team's despair and found refuge in the occasional home victory, coming out on top at the end of a long campaign still seemed to be beyond her. How could the Belles learn to dominate the game for the full period? Maybe it was the time of the month? Germaine couldn't believe her ears – tension might be mounting but she'd never let it get to her or the rest of the Belles. The answer wasn't in their heads, it was in their own hands or, more properly, their feet.

It was just the fillip that Germaine needed. The Belles stood their ground that day. Cosmetic changes to the side would have impressed nobody. They knew their destiny and now was the time to show everybody just what they were made of. It didn't matter if things turned ugly, they'd had a diet of defeat for longer than most of them cared to remember. Now was the time to start winning.

Naomi Wolf was free on the wing and with plenty of movement she looked the part, but the idea that this was going to be a beautiful game was a myth. Leave it to Jane Fonda if all you want is a work-out, Naomi's game was all about competing on a level playing field, fighting her way to the front to get a goal opportunity in the six-yard box. Spicy, these Belles weren't all saints as they mixed it in midfield to win that possession they'd fought for so tenaciously. They didn't care what shape their side was in, appearances weren't all they were cracked up to be – it was what you did in the here and now that mattered when it came to the crunch. And one thing was for sure, the Belles weren't taking it lying down. It wasn't in their vocabulary, as Dale Spender would no doubt remind them.

Up front they were serious. And there was no more need to iron things out at the back either. Their workrate was impressive, and they could all expect to be fully employed. Virginia Woolf had plenty of room to play her own way, while Valerie Solanas was great at cutting out balls. The Belles were in control, and that was just the way Germaine liked it.

Germaine convinced her players that there was nothing to fear from the change. They could afford those pregnant pauses on the ball to take things in their own time. They learnt to hold the game up – never mind their secondary role at the back, they were liberated finally from all that kind of stuff. Conscious of just what they could achieve, these Belles were destined for greater things. They had thought that, at number ten, Margaret Thatcher was the ultimate player, but Germaine taught them that they could achieve much more than even her. On a level playing field this team were more than a match for anyone, though the newfangled stadiums complete with glass ceilings did show there were still limits to their game. But even those structures couldn't hold the Belles back. They'd play a different game, separating the ball from between the other lot's legs. They had the desire to win and that was all that mattered. The signs were now there for all to see, and the Belles weren't going to let anyone else dominate the game. This wasn't simply about the physical side of things, but about control too. These Belles had the confidence to play as well away from home as the next man, and they knew they could give as good as they got. And if they had to labour to deliver, then that didn't mean the end of their careers either. It was their choice. Germaine had the positions sorted out at last. No more Belles complaining that their work was never done. 'Total football.' The whole woman, Germaine replied, and who could blame her.

Karl Marx

West Ham and Germany
Number 3 : Left-back

'The goal of which they are ignorant, what they cannot control, passes through a peculiar series of phases and stages independent of the will and actions of men.'

KARL MARX, *The German Ideology*

One of the commanding heights of any team he featured in, Karl Marx travelled far and wide before settling down with East London's West Ham. A Hammer through and through, Karl took a bit of a shine to the sickle too, but it didn't quite fit with the club crest.

Karl had played his way across Europe, a spectre looming over the pitch with his big, bushy beard and more than ample frame. The German, French and Belgian leagues were all witnesses to his skill but he just never quite fitted in. Left out and on his own, it was only England that he was able to call home. The first international, Karl was an original star, and read to boot.

Those who can, do, those who Kant, coach. That was how Karl introduced himself to the club trainer, Immanuel, who fancied himself as a tad enlightened. Immanuel was a big one for flair players, the lads who had it all and could turn a game all on their own. 'God's Gift' was what Immanuel called them, but he just couldn't find a way to prove their existence in the squad. Karl knew different; if that sort of player really did exist he'd probably be on opium, keeping the fans happy for now, but it would all end in tears as soon as the *News of the World* found out.

No big admirer of Kant then, but Karl did have more time for another of the club coaches, Hegel. Hegel reckoned those flair players weren't born but made. This kind of thinking was much more to Karl's liking. On such solid foundations the materials of a championship-winning team could be built. For Hegel, the team's future lay with his defence taking the battle to their tormentors, the other lot's forward line. Out on his left he placed young Ludwig Feuerbach, no big admirer of the divine right of your Arsenals, Man. Utds and Chelseas, to top the table, he denied their runs on his goal, time and time again. Karl's thesis was that Feuerbach had at least started to sort out the way to win.

Domestic talent lined up alongside Karl too. Out on the right Adam Smith was a free spirit, and when the ref wasn't looking his hidden hand would help the ball over the line. 'Goal!' cried his mate David Ricardo, a fellow right-sided player. Whilst bombing up and down the middle of the park, the Frenchman Proudhon and the Russian Bakunin paid little or no heed to the game's rules. But when things started to go missing in the changing-room, all eyes turned on this pair. 'All property is theft' was how they declared their innocence. Guilty, as charged , was the retort of the judge who sentenced them.

Karl admitted that he had had it up to here, as he tugged at his billowing beard. These players were deviating from the forward march that his labours down the left had marked out for them. Going nowhere, their adventurous runs would simply sap the strength of the team if he couldn't find a way to make things work. Karl's team-mate, Vladimir Ilyich Lenin, put it all down to youthful inexperience on their part. 'Infantile disorders' was how Lenin described the side's lesser and younger mortals out on the left wing.

Karl knew by now that simply exploiting the odd chance as it came his way wasn't the way to get anywhere. He had to accumulate some primitive talent of his own, and then go back to the raw basics of how not only to win the ball, but to keep it too. What was it that would keep the ball rolling towards goal? Many had sought an answer to that riddle, but none had found it. This was to be Karl's task, unlocking the laws of supplying the ball and satisfying the demands of those who wanted it in the back of the net. The young Marx had started off as a bit of an idealist in his search for his goal. He'd had faith in his coach, Hegel, in those early days. And Karl had appreciated the contribution of players like Isaac Newton. Isaac might not be able to defy the laws of gravity, but he did his best to win those iffy headers. And then there was Karl's fellow foreign import, René Descartes. A bit of a thinker, René was convinced of his place in the team. I play, therefore I am, and don't you just know it, René. But other teams soon found him out. He was all too predictable, playing to fixed formulas that were nigh-on mechanical in their delivery.

Spinoza was the next seemingly precocious talent to answer Karl's prayers, not that he believed in the spiritual, of course. Like Descartes, he was a system man, but he went further in freeing up the positions – just so long as there was a reason. But he didn't appreciate that things change, that what drove the team was all the players working together, not some dry and dusty match-winning formula. Karl started to look to others for inspiration – John Locke and David Hume offered some hope as a formidable pairing in central defence. Nothing was certain with those two around, as they found their own way to goal, free of any duty or responsibility to others.

Still Karl wasn't satisfied. Voltaire and Rousseau had their moments, but that Robespierre was a terror too much. Off with their heads, he would say. But then what use would a long ball be? Karl was running out of time, he had to find the formula that explained how some teams were winners while others always ended up on the losing side. The point was to change it. He had a scientific approach to the game that would surely stand him in good stead, yet he also understood that players couldn't just stand still, they had to move up and down the pitch as the ball moved from wing to wing, box to box.

'Dialectics' is what this nineteenth-century brainbox called his new system. Not to be confused with the charlatan in the space-cadet uniform, L. Ron Hubbard's 'Dianetics'. Nearly a hundred years before all those fancy-dan foreign coaches sullied the good old English game with their vitamin supplements, reflexology exercises and man-to-man talks about the inner self, Karl had found the answer, as the immovable force in the shape of a static back four shaped up to take on the irresistible object of a strapping six-foot-six old-fashioned number nine. Something surely had to give. And when it did, the outcome of the game would change. But this would only happen if the players were conscious of their capacity to win. They were still liable just to go through the motions. With their still-meagre wages in their back pockets, their hearts weren't in it. They were producing the goods all right down on the pitch, but what did they have to show for it? Nowt. Not players, just numbers, production-line performers robbed of their individuality and ability. 'Dialectics, dire-electrics!' The witty forebears of Eric Hall and his cigar-chomping like weren't so impressed with Karl's promise of change as they wittily put down his well-thought-out innovations. The struggle continues, the thoughtful Karl mused.

That's capital. Wages, prices, profit were the answer as Karl carefully scripted a way out of this sad state of affairs. His downtrodden mates owned nothing but their boots and kit, they had neither the means nor the ends to win the game for themselves. But they did have the legs to run the line, the feet that could poke the ball through a hapless keeper's legs, the heads to connect with a cross of rifle-shot accuracy, the hands that miraculously stretched to stop a ball that seemed certain to condemn them to last-minute defeat. These were properties no one else could own and were way too valuable to put a price on either.

Distribution was all. In the centre of midfield the Frenchman Babeuf conspired to spread the ball to all four corners of the pitch. And his fellow countrymen Saint-Simon and Fourier, though hardly scientific in their approach on goal, did at least have the rudiments of a plan. But it was when Karl persuaded his mate Fred Engels to join him from his wet Wednesdays spent in faraway Manchester that their game really began to take off.

Engels' condition was pure class. He'd profit from others' mistakes, dictating the pace of the game, securing the means to produce goals. He was never surplus to requirements, nobody could put a price on his value to the team. Exchange him? Never.

Under the combined leadership of Marx and Engel, the players massed in the middle of the park. Concentrated at the point of production, the halfway line was covered in claret-and-blue shirts. 'C'mon you Irons,' the shout went up, the crowd impatient for movement. 'Don't lumpen it at 'em,

though,' Karl countenanced. Do that and you'll never be sure how things might turn out. The patient build up was best, combining a union of head and body neatly. No longer slaves to the rhythm of the game, they held their destiny in their own boots. They were determined to win and, being economic with the ball, victory at last seemed a certainty. But nothing in football, as Karl was soon to discover, is inevitable. His great rival Charles Darwin had barely survived with the fittest of sides; they'd evolved into a club of mid-table no-hopers. Would this be Karl's fate too?

Karl had the base of a very good team, of that he was certain. The superstructure left a bit to be desired, but he had ideas for that too. After all, a critique of the Gotha programme on a European away leg had even led to improvements in the club's own matchday magazine.

As for tactics, it was all becoming about time and space. Take your time on the ball, then win yourself some space. Nothing elaborate, mind you, the movement remained key. Liberal passing of the ball was no good, and certainly not very productive. There were only two routes on goal, down the left or the right, with nothing of consequence happening in the centre of the park. The side was now in such a state that it dominated the pitch, though Karl remained anxious that, fragile souls as they were, they might just wither away. Of course he had an army of reserves should they falter, but that just didn't seem fair. And as for monopolising the middle ground, that was a tactic he'd leave to others.

And then Karl came up against Dühring – a fellow German and master tactician. If Karl could get the Hammers past this tricky encounter he knew they'd be okay for ever more. As the two sides battled it out, Karl rearranged his players and at last it all began to make sense. Man-for-man marking meant he could cancel the other lot out. Negative against negative, he would use the players he had stacked up in his five-man midfield to release some quality balls into the box. Their opposite numbers wouldn't know what had hit them and victory was Karl's.

But Karl knew that time didn't stand still. He introduced

Eduard Bernstein to run down the right-wing and, soon enough, Bernstein was re-writing the script as he revised the line-up. With a second international, Kautsky, providing more orthodox cover down the left, the pairing was unbeatable for a while. But again it wasn't to last. On a long away trip to the Finland Station, the costly import, Lenin, joined them once more from the guard's van. A professional, he seemed to be the spark the side needed, but no one would be taking any liberties any more, that much was certain. For Marx, however, works completed, he knew that West Ham United now had nothing to lose but their games.

Dmitri Shostakovich

Zenit Leningrad and Soviet Union
Number 4 : Central Midfield

DMITRI SHOSTAKOVICH, 'Football', Opus 66
(Second Movement)

Футбол

Dmitri Shostakovich composed himself. At number four, he was the centre of a quartet of midfield dynamos, even though he much preferred the lesser-known Zenit team of Leningrad to their Moscow betters. Dmitri could run the legs off most defences as he produced the passes to release his forwards.

On song, Shostakovich was a joy to watch; committed in the tackle, his career was a testimony to sacrifice. The player who notched up the assists never quite got the glory of scoring goals, but his contribution was vital all the same. Dmitri was a realist, most of the time, and as a bit of a party man, social all of the time. Labouring away in the middle of the park he had his moments, and camped out on the halfway line he never did lose his concentration. He left that to Sakharov and Solzhenitsyn, who were always going in the book for dissent. But the one-man show that the game was always in danger of becoming wasn't much to Dmitri's liking either. Big Joe Stalin certainly had his admirers, but all this cult of the personality stuff was getting out of hand –

whatever next, *Hello* front covers and Brylcreem adverts? Dmitri was probably lucky enough not to be playing in the era of Becks and Posh.

Managers knew that, with Dmitri, they had a player they could rely on. He was always happy enough to be a sounding board for new tactics: modern one week, a *Libero* playing a free role just behind the front two, then back to a more traditional four–four–two the next. Chopping and changing the composition of the team, Dmitri took it all in his loping stride. Dependable, certainly, but an artist on the ball in his own right too, he was rarely out of tune with the needs of the rest of his team, conducting their successful forays towards goal from deep in his own half. And, boy, could he dish it out if the team looked like conceding a sloppy goal. 'The pits!' he would angrily cry out when his attempt to orchestrate a fast-moving break went wrong and the Leningrad defence were caught short on a counter-attack. Back from the front, star forward and team captain, Joe Stalin, insisted that the team could withstand any siege, but Dmitri was able to spot the gaps in their defensive wall that would eventually be his side's undoing.

Pointing out the weaknesses in the defence didn't do Dmitri any favours with the team's success-starved fans. They'd been queuing round the block for more seasons than most of them would care to remember just to see their side on top of the pile. But with a side built on such fragile foundations, Dmitri remained to be convinced that success would be theirs in the end. For now, though, he was happy enough keeping just on the pitch as he toed the touchline, patrolling this vital part of their half with a menacing look and a hoof of a kick to match. Clearing the ball upfield, he knew that, for now at least, he could keep the threat of defeat at bay. But for how long? Dmitri sadly wondered as he confined himself to this solitary role. Stalin wasn't having any of this, 'Up and at 'em.' He demanded that Dmitri and the rest of the players throw themselves into the attack, whatever they had to sacrifice at the back. Goals for were always better than goals against as Stalin set out to rewrite the history books.

Dmitri was the kind of player who worried constantly over his performances. When the game seemed to turn against him he queried his own position – stuck in midfield, maybe he was thinking things through too formally, treating his role as a ball-winner too rigidly. The monotony of just humping the ball skywards was starting to get to him. He wanted to get into the channels, make the odd sublime pass. But Stalin wasn't having any of this, and all this dainty footwork did nothing to convince him that Dmitri was doing anything more than just fidgeting with the ball. 'Service, that's what we need, service!' Stalin bellowed. And Dmitri seemed to have no choice but to obey.

Driving the ball forward, Dmitri knew that he could at

least give the team a certain rhythm to their play. It might be instrumental, but if the ball ended up in the back of the net who was complaining? 'You only sing when you're winning' the opposition's fans would chant at Dmitri. Well, what was wrong with that, he wondered? Stalin was with Dmitri on this one all the way, he had nothing against a touch of instrumentalism, and for that much Dmitri was relieved. Like Ivan before him, Joe could be terrible if he got on your back, so having Joe on your side was reward enough in itself. Passing the ball from left to right and back again, the team cleared their lines with ruthless efficiency and moved forward in harmony. This was the movement that Dmitri had been hoping for, and as the clock ticked towards the ninetieth minute he knew in his heart the crashing crescendo of a last-minute winner was theirs for the taking.

With another victory snatched at the very end of the game, the team had a certain gathering momentum about them; just the way Dmitri liked it. And now he started to pull some strings as he trumpeted the club's achievement to anyone who would listen. He needed to bring in some new players, there weren't enough virtuoso performers to keep their title challenge going all season long. Playing solo up front, he knew his centre-forward would eventually be found wanting. The odd unexpected turn was what he was looking for, haunting and menacing, a player who would draw defenders out of the box before spinning the ball elegantly into the top corner.

Dmitri took a long, hard look at the playing staff he now had at his disposal to see what his options were. Vivaldi was good enough for four seasons, but after that, what use was he? That Johann Strauss could waltz through most defences but his performances off the ball were frankly hopeless. Then there were plenty who reckoned Handel was the Messiah they'd all been waiting for, but Dmitri wasn't so ready to sing his praises. Still his search went on. Mozart was a bit too cosy in his attitude to the game for Dmitri's hard-working liking, but then Beethoven was deaf to almost every conceivable insult anyone would throw at him. No oik in the stands was going to put him off his game.

Maybe, just maybe, Dmitri could make something out of these very different talents, but they'd all have to learn that Stalin would only promise them one party. No rabble-rousing all season long. That's why Dmitri had to offload the hard-drinking Liszt, who in his wake gave his name to a habit plenty more players would take up after him. Brahms and Liszt, a partnership not made in heaven, Dmitri decided. Absolutely, vodka and the rest would be ruled out of the refreshments list henceforth.

With Rossini, Dmitri thought his search for a 30-goal-a-season man up front might finally be over. A bit of a lone ranger and with a Christian name like Gioachino, he certainly sounded like the kind of player you could build a side around. So now Dmitri could really get down to business. A man to slip past defenders was what he needed next. Well, the promising newcomer, Andrew Lloyd Webber, was so slick he was more phantom than player; no wonder everyone reckoned he was a superstar in the making. And if you wanted a tough tackler then Tchaikovsky was your man to crack nuts. 'Sweet,' Stalin grimly agreed, as another crumpled forward ended up at Tchaikovsky's feet.

Out on the right, Dmitri put Richard Wagner – he'd run rings round anyone. It was a controversial signing. Dmitri thought Stalin would prefer his wingers to run down the left but Joe didn't seem to mind where they played, it was all the same to him, only the end result mattered.

Elgar would promenade on the edge of the box, more in hope than glory, but an imposing figure all the same. He was constantly caught offside which was more of a problem. And the ref rarely missed a note in his book as he took his name. Not such a perfect pitch with all these suspensions mounting up, Dmitri thought, so he had little option but to rest Elgar for a few games.

But his substitute Debussy was scarcely much better. A Frenchman, it was maybe not such a big surprise that he'd be a brooding, moody kind of guy in the Emmanuel Petit mould. But who would have thought that the Austrian Schoenberg would also be so out of tune with what Dmitri was trying to achieve? Poor old Dmitri mistakenly thought he was signing a mild-mannered Central European-type on the cheap.

Shipping these two out, Dmitri replaced them with the two Gustavs: Mahler, who had the pace to last a long game and well into extra time if that was what was required, and Holst, who was so good he was on another planet.

Surely Stalin would now be satisfied? This was a team that really could compete with the best. But Joe had other plans and poor Dmitri was once again in danger of falling out of favour. Dmitri tried everything to keep the side on track to the top. He put together a great sequence with victory following victory. A treble even looked a realistic possibility. The team had a base, but were sharp too. Their performances certainly weren't flat and they had the tempo to beat just about anyone who came their way. But still Stalin wasn't satisfied. So, in desperation, Dmitri tried jazzing things up with Ellington and Gershwin but that really sent him plummeting in Stalin's estimation. 'Back to basics,' Joe grimly demanded. Poor Dmitri had thought a touch of transatlantic flair was the right ingredient to open up a second front as the team challenged for cup and league honours, but Joe was anything but impressed.

So, no more improvisation, and experimentation was out too. Stalin wanted things kept simple; teams packed with utility players was how he liked it. Shostakovich could see that this was to be the new status quo, but he hardly expected the team to rock the world if they played like this. Dmitri knew by now that being bolshie got you nowhere with Stalin so he buckled down to work once more with his side. Stravinsky and Prokofiev were given free transfers – out on a limb, they'd already been exiled to the bench. Dmitri also knew that, unless he turned things around, he'd be out on his ear with them in next to no time. He struggled for a while but he then unearthed a real gem in Dostoevsky. Miserable as sin, his career up to now had been a right tragedy in the making, but Stalin took a liking to his traditional way with the ball and Dmitri thought he could maybe fashion a new side out of the mess he'd unwittingly created for himself.

Twisting and turning, Stalin didn't mind his players adopting the most unpredictable positions – just so long as the end product was a goal. Finally, Dmitri had a grasp of what Stalin was after. He could afford to be unpredictable in his selections if the results went in their favour. And, as he started to produce the goods, his stock certainly rose with the naturally suspicious Stalin. Rachmaninov was brought in to perform a double role, solo performer but also composing the side ready for when the other lot might try to break forward from a set piece. A homegrown player, this was more to Stalin's liking; he'd grown tired of all those internationals. Shostakovich now began to perform at breakneck speed, so fast that the rest of the side could barely keep up with him. He tried to conduct them in how he expected them to perform but they were still struggling, and a few players would have to go. The hard labours that Stalin had put them through on the training ground had simply sapped their strength and the end-of-season clearout was more like a purge, as the list of free transfers to lower-division sides mounted up.

Dmitri was feeling bolder again. Cap in hand, he went to Stalin and asked for some brass. Quality players didn't come cheap. Stalin wasn't stupid, he could see that. Dmitri had drummed up a lot of support for his plan. 'I'll give you five years,' Stalin declared through gritted teeth, as he handed over the roubles. Dmitri knew that, compared to Joe, Deadly Doug Ellis and Cuddly Ken Bates were a pushover, and he'd have to deliver, make no mistake about that.

No more fiddling around, then, as Dmitri asked his side to give him their performance of a lifetime. They'd need to leave the opposition standing, and rumour had it that that was the least Stalin expected of them. Dmitri added more strength to his side. 'Stakhanov's mine!' he shouted uncharacteristically, punching the air with his fists as he celebrated the addition of this hard-working midfielder who he knew would labour until the very end for a victory. The new signing did seem to be what the side had been looking for. With Stakhanov in the starting line-up, Dmitri's team now led the rest of the clubs on a right song and dance. And their shots against the wall found their targets too. Stalin couldn't have been happier. 'You're murdering them,' Stalin exclaimed, and that's just what he wanted, too. Dmitri, by this point, knew though that this wasn't the side that he'd hoped for; they didn't play the game the way he liked it, they were anything but classical. But when Stalin turned to him to ask, 'You know the score, don't you?' Dmitri knew that, sadly, he had little choice but to agree.

Søren Kierkegaard

FC Copenhagen and Denmark
Number 5 : Central Defender

'*The individual is forever quite close to the goal and the same moment at a distance from it.*'

SØREN KIERKEGAARD, *Either/Or*

Søren Kierkegaard was one of the few Danish players of any quality to stick at home instead of trying to make it big as a cheap export that an English league manager might come to regret. No John Jensen-style disasters for Søren Kierkegaard, and certainly no dodgy brown envelopes coming his agent's way either. Instead, except for a brief move to Berlin, he chose to make his mark with his hometown club, FC Copenhagen.

Enigmatic is a word often used to describe those quietly spoken Scandinavian types who play it dour but hanker after the 'Søren the Viking' chants that greet their all-too-rare goals. It's as if a great weight has been lifted from their shoulders as a darting run from midfield finally ends with the ball in the back of the net instead of the top row of the stands. Handstands and backflips, shirt over the head, running to the corner flag to give it a tug before diving headfirst across the grass, waiting expectantly for a pile of team-mates' bodies to land about his ears. Oh yes, those

Danes know how to let their flaxen hair down! Probably the best goal ever scored? Well, maybe.

Søren was as enigmatic as the best of them. An individual who stood out in any squad, his mission in the game wasn't just to find the ball but to find himself. This could make for a bit of a lonely kind of fellow, always going on and on about his own precious self. Not exactly Number One on your party guest list, Søren wasn't one to prop yourself up next to at the post-match lager session either. It took his coaches a while to unlock his particular contribution to the team, but when they did they began to realise that in their ranks they had a genius who needed careful nurturing if he was to become a real asset to the side.

It came as a mild surprise, then, that Søren was a bit of a ladies' man on the sly. Splashed all over the Danish tabloids, 'Diary of a Seducer', 'My Steamy Nights of Passion with Søren the Super Stud', 'Centre-Half Fails to Score at the Altar' – Søren's long-time girlfriend, tall and leggy Regina Olsen kissed and told of Søren breaking off their engagement. There was no hiding place on the pitch for sad Søren and soon enough his game went to pieces.

Luckily, the Berlin University side came in for him. Their youth team, the Young Hegelians, needed to strengthen their defensive spine and Søren fitted the bill perfectly. Glad to be out of the limelight for a while, Søren teamed up with Friedrich Engels, Ludwig Feuerbach and Mikhail Bakunin to start to piece together a team that might one day cast a spectre over European competition. But this was still some time in the future, and Søren was a man in a hurry. So when the din had died down back home in Denmark he was mighty glad to make a comeback with his beloved FC Copenhagen. Now that the spurned Regina was no longer on the scene, Søren was at last able to find the time to concentrate on putting his game back together again.

With a cup run unfolding, Søren was full of fear. The indignity of falling victim to a lower-division side raising their game for the big city flash-boys of Copenhagen was ever present. His knees were all atremble, though not having the poetic flair of Ossie Ardilles, he never did find a rhyming couplet to turn his nerves into a terrace classic. Still, with a weak back, a stoop and skinny legs, Søren had more than enough to worry about without bothering to track down Chas and Dave to knock out a dodgy song for Copenhagen's moment of cup glory.

His return to the side wasn't the spectacular success he'd hoped for either. The memory of Regina's exposure of their nights of passion might have been receding into the fans' memory, but until Søren started to deliver on the park he'd still be cutting a sorry figure in the middle of the team's defence. He knew he had the answer to his predicament at his feet, but passing the ball forwards was never his strongest point. If he could just pass it back to some giant of a goalie who was bellowing at his back for it – Peter Schmeichel being only the latest in a long line of loud-mouthed Danish titans between the sticks – Søren would do so every time, just for an easy life. But caution didn't exactly endear you to your forwards who were screaming out for some service. Poor old Søren couldn't win, whatever he did.

He had to break with the responsibilities of being a team player; it just wasn't right the way he was expected to please everybody all of the time. The needs of the players behind him simply weren't the same as the lads up front. If he was to help them both out then he needed to have the time and the space to play the game the way he wanted to play it.

Barking out instructions, Søren began to come into his own as he visibly grew in confidence. Gone was the stoop, as he rushed forward to stand tall on the edge of the box as the lobbed ball from an indirect free-kick came his way. Glancing off his forehead, the ball went goalwards; Søren had found his goal. The aura of gloom that had been all around him began to ebb away.

The game, he realised, wasn't really so complicated after all. Getting the simple things right was how he'd become a more complete player, the fancy-dan stuff he'd leave to the costly Brazilian imports – not that you saw too many of your Ronaldos and Rivaldos in the Danish league. Coming up for corners and set-pieces, Søren knew that so long as he could lose his marker then the ability to leap high into the sky was more often than not enough to put the ball away where it belonged – over the other lot's goalline. This was what football was all about, 1–0 to the Copenhagen and never mind the style. Playing to impress was all well and good, but it was the score at the end of ninety minutes that really mattered. Søren was interested in concrete results and never mind how his side secured them.

All this individualism, however, wasn't based on a surplus of skill with the ball at their feet. Each of the Copenhagen players was left to find his own route to goal, but with none of that dribbling along the way, drifting left and right with a shimmy here and a nutmeg there. Though they were determined to score, the dread of not scoring imposed an overbearing caution on their play. They defended deep, forcing themselves back into their own space, retreating behind the run of play, finding themselves gathered around the ball – this was how Copenhagen ground out all those 0–0 draws. But one point was better than none, Kierkegaard would preach, at least they'd got something out of the game. No points was nothing compared to that solitary point that lifted them above the relegation zone. And just so long as they did that then the club would always survive in the top flight. Nothing spectacular would be achieved, but this dogged determination to exist alongside the bigger clubs was something in itself to hold on to. And grimly holding on was what Kierkegaard's Copenhagen were all about.

Søren had his own objectives too, of course. He wanted to find out what made this game of football tick. He tested out tactical masterplan after tactical masterplan, trying to find an answer. How to score and to lift his club into the top half of the table, this became his subject. This wouldn't be done by facts and figures alone, Søren found. The tried-and-tested formulas of success lacked the pride and the passion that he knew was what inspired even the modestly gifted to greater things. And as Søren began to come into his own as an individual unit in a team of individuals not squad numbers, his value soared. But this being pre-Bosman he was never

going to make a mint out of his now undoubted ability.

Seeing his name on the scoresheet, the author of his own success, that would be more than enough reward for Søren. But if too many games went by without Søren putting the goals away, he knew his value to the side would sink as rapidly as it had risen. Football was a risky enterprise, the anguish and anxiety of missing only ever the thickness of a goalpost or crossbar away. The dividing line between success and failure not much more than a handful of inches, or centimetres in the case of metric Denmark.

Knowing that his playing career could die an early death at any time kept Søren on his toes. This could also make him a touch morbid in the dressing-room before the big kick-off. Strangers to the side, like Albert Camus, could find this put them off their own matchday preparations to start with. But facing up to the possibility of defeat, they soon found, helped to equip them for the miracle of victory. The doom and gloom was best banished by a right romping victory over bitter rivals Brondby.

Either they'd come out on top or not. The choice was that of the players alone. Each and every one of them would have their own personal battle with their opposite number, and the sum of those battles would determine the match's outcome. It was all well and good having the solid foundations that the likes of Galileo and Copernicus could give you, with their science of football by passing the ball up the centre, but if the rest of the side weren't fully conscious then the passes would simply go to waste. Full of self-belief, Søren was more aware than most of the need to keep your eyes open for a ball coming your way. But for all that positive thinking, he was racked with doubt too. Keeping body and soul together wasn't so easy when your passes went awry, you'd lost your final touch and you were at least a yard off the pace. No wonder on a bad day his team-mates reckoned Søren had a death wish, as another hopeless lunge saw him give a penalty away in the closing minutes of the game.

'Suicidal, that's what he is,' the lads ruminated as they watched their goalkeeper go the wrong way. But that fateful lunge had been born out of a passion, a will to win whatever the costs. Defiant to the last, Søren was more determined than ever to make amends. With only stoppage time remaining, he remembered the dour German type, Martin Luther, who'd pinned up the team sheet that morning. 'I have a dream,' Søren yelled at the bench. 'Bring Martin Luther on and I'll make a king of him.' Absurd, surely, but Copenhagen hardly had anything to lose at 1–0 down and defeat staring them in the face. 'What shall I do?' the startled Luther asked of Søren. 'Choose yourself,' Søren tartly replied as he kicked off. A headlong rush to goal was Luther's choice and, as the ball sailed through the air, all the moves they'd so religiously practised on the training ground finally fell into place. Luther trapped the ball on the edge of the area and cheekily lobbed it out to his left. Søren had charged into this position and, wild-eyed, he leapt forward. Deranged wasn't the word for it. Two big and burly full-backs were bearing down on him but somehow he connected with the ball just inches, sorry millimetres, ahead of their boots. Søren was free at last, he was lost in the heap of bodies but he'd gained the space he needed, and with just the one foot free of all that heaving humanity he volleyed the ball into the top corner. He'd found his goal, and on that score, 1–1, he was happy at last to be judged.

George Orwell

Wigan Athletic and England
Number 6 : Central Defender

'*Football . . . has nothing to do with fair play. It is bound up with hatred, jealousy, boastfulness, disregard of all rules and sadistic pleasure in witnessing violence. In other words, it is war minus the shooting.*'

GEORGE ORWELL, *Tribune*, 1945

Even though he was a naturally left-sided player, George Orwell found that there were plenty who struggled to read his game. He was put in the centre for much of his career, he led with his left but he could do a job on the right too, so the middle of the pitch did seem the best place for him.

George was one of the first of his generation to make it big in Europe; when he turned up in Barcelona they came from far and wide to pay homage in Catalonia. And once that particular adventure was over, George headed back to the land of the lion and the unicorn, England. He thought his reputation would have gone before him. After all, in Paris and on his return to London, George provided the defensive cover for big-city sides in danger of ending up down-and-out on the relegation scrapheap. His style was more airstrip one than route one, as he lofted the ball skywards, rushing upfield to catch the other lot unawares with his aerial bombardment of the penalty area, a technique he'd originally observed at first hand in Spain. But the little-Englanderism he encountered back home gave little or no weight to these new-fangled continental ideas, and even when he pointed to the title-winning team he'd put together during some days in faraway Burma there were few who were impressed. He found himself farmed out, a division or two below the playing level he was used to, where the defenders had a tendency to play like animals.

He didn't complain, though, as setting the aspidistras flying – let alone the half-time teacups – wasn't his style. But he remained a bit of a rabble-rouser, and once he'd settled in with his new side, George took the lads to one side to tell them a tale that was pure fantasy football. He told them of a vision that an old mate of his, nicknamed The Major because he was a bit of a midfield general, had passed on to him. This wizened old geezer had a dream team in his head where everyone in the side would have their part to play. There'd be no more go-it-alone glory-seekers hurtling down the wing but losing out with their final touch; cart-horses and donkeys would be as vital to the team as the centre-forwards who could climb head and shoulders above the rest to head the ball unerringly into the back of the net. And most important of all, the rewards that came with these goals would be shared out equally amongst all the players. Why should the manager and the club's directors cream off all the fruits of what was going on down on the pitch? They were keen enough to tuck into the profit that came their way after another giant-killing cup run or promotion, but it wasn't the board or the loudmouth shouting his head off from the bench who scored the goals, put in the tackles and made the saves that earned those victories. It was all take, take, take. And what did the players have to look forward to? Knackered and washed up, there wasn't anything left for them once their playing days were over – apart from running a pub and the odd afternoon out on the golf course rounded off with a dose of the goals that got away.

All this rabble-rousing had a tendency to go in one ear and out the other. So the Major turned his philosophising into a chant, *The Players of England*, that was soon destined to become a terrace classic: 'The people's game is coming home, chairman and board will be overthrown, the playing fields are ours to roam, and the victories will be ours alone'. Dodgy rhyming couplets notwithstanding, the players were impressed. This people's game lark was catching.

But George reminded his spellbound listeners that having hope in your heart wasn't enough, you had to have organisation too. The tale of the Major had made its biggest impact, song and all, on the most pig-headed members of the old boy's team, Snowy and Boney – the shortening of his first name Napoleon to 'Nappy' had been too much for the poor dear to bear. You couldn't go around sounding like a soon-to-be-soiled item of a baby's underwear and strike the fear of God into the opposition, could you? The Major wasn't so sure of Snowy and Boney's best intentions but he knew that together they had the potential to be a match-winning combination. Snowy was inventive and quick-witted whilst Boney was the kind of player used to getting his own way – pushing and shoving, he was too much of a handful for most defenders. Together they led the line and, come Saturday, they were well up for showing the board who was really boss. As the chairman and his fat-cat pals basked in the well-fed afterglow of another hard-fought victory, Snowy and Boney were plotting. First, they tore off the hated shoddy sponsors' logos that had spoilt what was once a classic strip; next they chucked out the dreaded weights machine from their much-loved boot-room. Endless sessions of pumping iron had come to replace the cherished blackboard-and-chalk team talks which should have turned out a side of craftsmen of the ball rather than the muscle-bound metronomes that they threatened to become. The racket the crashing weights caused soon alerted the manager and chairman that something was amiss, but it was too late. The boardroom doors burst open, and in an instant the players had delivered their boots to a target they could hardly miss: the ample behinds of those who had come to run the club in their own selfish interest.

George's team-mates were spellbound by this story. They thought that they could read him like a book but here was a player with real strength in depth. Soon enough he gave the lads their next instalment. 'Player-power' was what Snowy and Boney were about. For them and their team-mates, anyone who sat on their haunches was an enemy. Up on your feet – fans and players alike – and you were a friend. There'd be no more big, ugly, mock-Tudor homes in the suburbs either, no drinking and betting binges, no fouling, and all because they were to treat each other as equals. The following Saturday the terraces were full of good cheer as the chant rang out around the stadium: 'Stand up and you're good, sit down and you're bad'. The opposition's directors looked distinctly uncomfortable as they sat down to that particular, and raucously loud, ditty.

The first game under player-power went well enough, too. Though it was soon noted that both Boney and Snowy had developed an uncanny knack of leading from behind while grabbing all the glory. They weren't exactly in the thick of the action when it came to tackling back or scrapping for the loose ball in the opposition's penalty area. Still, when the whistle blew for full-time, with three points safely in the bag, the team knew in their hearts that they'd won for themselves that day and not for the manager, the directors or, least of all, the chairman. And that was all that seemed to matter.

More victories came and went. Much of the credit was down to an old cart-horse at the back, Boxer. He was hardly graceful but he carried the team through those tough times when nothing much seems to go right. Hoofing the ball safely back to where it had come from, he'd pull his defenders together and dig deep for one final push through to the ninetieth minute. And if anyone faulted his contribution, Boxer had one simple retort: 'I will work harder,' a tyro to the last. It was heavy going, not just for Boxer either. The whole side had to work together as one, but once the game was over at least they had their Sunday of rest to look forward to.

But, ominously, at the centre of the midfield, Snowy and Boney's partnership was starting to break up and there was a very real danger of that precious team spirit ebbing away as the rows got worse and worse. Snowy and Boney had set up shop together in the boot-room. From here they were to issue the tactical masterplans that would see their side to victory. Snowy had found that he preferred the odd trot around the training ground rather than being cooped up in the liniment-soaked atmosphere of the boot-room. Left to his own devices, Boney took charge of the youth team, drilling his charges in secret routines day after day as they perfected their one party piece for those precious free-kick opportunities.

The lads who'd stuck around to hear George's tale this far were breathless with excitement, they could hardly wait to hear what happened next. 'What is to be done?' they cried out. Now that was half the problem, George explained, as his story unfolded.

Challenging for Europe, this player-power-inspired eleven were besieged by their big-time rivals, City and United. If they only worked together to take maximum points from Snowy and Boney's lot and settled for a draw between themselves then the top two spots would be City and United's for the taking. But they just couldn't get on with each other and any chance of co-operation seemed right out of the question. Not to worry, they thought, this player-power will be just another five-minute wonder, like coloured boots, bubble perms and those number tags tucked into your socks that Don Revie reckoned would change the face of modern football.

The white shirts of United were the first to challenge Boney and Snowy's outfit on their home ground. Snowy sorted out his defence. A draw was the best he reckoned they could hope for. He marked out the positions, the defence staying well back, hardly venturing out of their own half. The midfield, meanwhile, were snapping at the heels of United's forwards, shoving them from one side to the other, never letting them settle on the ball. On the break, the forwards charged headlong into United's penalty area, while Boxer came up from the back, laying out anyone who tried to take the ball off him as he almost walked it over the line. Boxer couldn't share in his side's joy, though, as the cry of 'GOAAAAL!' went up. He really had laid one of the other lot out, the trainer couldn't raise him, and the poor guy would have to be stretchered off. Boxer was still trying to come to terms with the terrible deed he'd done as they kicked off again. So consumed with guilt was he that he didn't even notice the crafty beggar slipping back on to the pitch from the touchline, fit enough to play again once he'd realised his dramatic fall to the ground had failed to land Boxer with a red card. Snowy shouted at poor old Boxer to drop the sentimental stuff, the game was there to be won and whatever it took to get those three points was worth it, never mind the cost in bookings and injuries.

With hard , fought-out games like this earning the team the grudging respect of their enemies, this was going to be a long season. Snowy continued to come up with all sorts of ways to improve the playing side of things, whilst Boney didn't appear to have any ideas of his own and kept coming back to the need to produce the goods in the box. Without balls to their feet the forwards would starve; the lines of supply were vital, or so Boney claimed.

Snowy had a master plan all of his own. Miller was his name, not unnaturally nicknamed Windy Miller, a hugely creative, attacking midfielder who would be the missing cog in their championship-challenging machine, the fourth international to give the hard-pressed squad a bit of extra capacity. With his skill on the ball, some of the players would be able to sit back and take it easy for the odd game, no more hurtling up and down the length of the pitch. Windy would cut out the workload with the rapier-like accuracy of his passing game. Boney was distinctly unimpressed by this proposal. The fancy footwork might impress some but not him. Goal production was all: the percentage game was the one sure way to grind out the victories, not costly imports. They had their targets and they should stick to them. And when push came to shove, Boney was not a big one for the old pals' act. Snowy found himself substituted, replaced by young pups of players whom Boney had so carefully nurtured until they were ready to make their debut. Snowy was out of favour, exiled from the team. Betrayed, he went off and played his way around the continental leagues, first entering one side labouring up the

table then another, before settling eventually in Mexico. But this was no happy hunting ground either – he'd once been a medal winner but now he couldn't even make his local side, picked on as a loser rather than enjoying the fruits of victory he had worked so hard to make happen.

George, by this stage of his recitation-marathon, was clean out of breath. He needed to come up for some air but the lads were egging him on for more. And so the story entered its final phase. Boney taught the side to play out their games for dire 0–0 draws: a point won was, for him, better than a point dropped. Boxer held the back together, consoling himself that, with clean sheet following clean sheet, the gaffer – as Boney now insisted on people calling him – was always right.

Then, much to the lads' amazement, Boney put in a bid for the self-same Windy Miller that he'd so effectively rubbished when Snowy had suggested buying him just a season or two ago. The change of mind was put down to tactics, the mysteries of which the players never did fully comprehend. Having bought Windy, Boney stunned the lads still further by announcing that this was the start of a selling spree. The team spirit of player-power was no more, they were just pieces of meat to be traded to the highest bidder. Things would never be the same again, a sentiment all too quickly confirmed when Boney was spotted gladhanding it in the old boardroom with sponsors, directors and their sordid like. Was this what player-power had come to?

On the pitch Boney was building a side of ball-winners, no more passing the ball around, and those that refused to lay the ball off to his tough-tackling midfielders would in turn be starved of service. He also knew the value of getting your retaliation in first – they were to be ruthless in the tackle whilst putting the opposition's six-yard box under siege and looking for any goalmouth opening. All the earlier disappointments of mid-table mediocrity were purged from the memory.

Pretenders to Boney's gaffership came and went. They'd show up for a trial but Boney soon saw them off as he continued to lead from behind in his own, fortunately, unique style. Five years is how long Boney planned it would take to capture the championship, and plenty would fall by the wayside on the way there. Boxer was one who stayed the course of his defensive duties longer than most, but when he could no longer carry the side he was knackered. Once the lads had dreamed of a nice, cosy retirement home in the Benidorm or Florida sun with a golf course attached. Now it was just the ignominy of playing your way down the divisions until you were too old even for that.

Boney taught his side that true happiness was only to be found through hard graft. But strange to tell, as he bullied his team-mates into greater and huger physical efforts, Boney's own playing contribution became less and less. He was putting on more than a bit of weight and he had a liking for a post-match tipple or three. He was still registered as a player, but his appearances on the pitch were few and far between. His appetite for victory was as keen as ever, of course, it's just that he didn't like sharing in the work that earned those precious points.

What had begun as the Major's dream team had turned into a particularly nasty nightmare. George didn't have much left to tell the lads now. As for himself, he could feel a big-money transfer coming on, though when he peered into the papers he learnt it was lowly Wigan Athletic after all. There was just one more final twist to his tale that he wanted to tell before he was gone up the motorway.

Towards the end of his career, Boney was caught in the tunnel for one of those instant interviews after the game. Asked to justify his bulging waistline and soaring salary, he angrily retorted: 'All players are equal at this club, but some players are more equal than others.' The fans were as loyal as ever and, realising that their gaffer was hardly ever off the bench or out of the Director's Box nowadays, echoed these self-same sentiments with their new chant: 'Standing's good, sittings's better.' Player-power had come full circle, the people's game would have to wait for another champion. Boney's Big Brother offered his services for the 1983–84 season, but George said that was another story.

Niccolò Machiavelli

Fiorentina and Italy
Number 7 : Outside-right

---

*'Each succeeds in reaching the goal by a
different method.'*

NICCOLÒ MACHIAVELLI, *The Prince*

Niccolò Machiavelli, the player formerly known as Prince, held the Fiorentina midfield together throughout his long career, apart from the odd spell with the big-city boys of Roma. A tough-tackling right-winger, he cast fear into any lily-livered opponent who had to face the forlorn task of trying to get past him down the channels. Ball-winning was his speciality, while issuing a stream of instructions to those inside him to hold their positions tight so an attack down the middle could be mounted.

There were plenty who wouldn't trust the none-too-ironically nicknamed 'Old Nick' as far as they could throw him. Betrayed by him, siding with the board when it suited him or providing juicy leaks to the local *Gazetta della Sport* scribes, managers fell out with Nick thick and fast. But just so long as the results were going his way, Nick's place in the team would be safe enough. When winning ways turned to losing, though, Nick found himself condemned to the stiffs sooner than you could say 'Machiavellian, eh?' – with an accompanying outward stretch of the hands and Godfather-like shrug of the padded shoulders. But exile was an indignity Nick vowed he wouldn't suffer for long.

At his best, cynical was how most commentators described Nick's approach to football – studs up, elbows flailing, knee in the other poor sod's groin. As long as the team won then the odd broken limb was a small penalty for an opponent to pay. The end-of-the-season spoils were more than enough to justify the means that got the team there – though treatment rooms throughout the Serie A might not agree.

Nick knew what he was after: a Fiorentina side at the top of the pile, and he wasn't too bothered how he took them there. Putting one over AC and Inter Milan, Juventus and Lazio, revenge could be sweet, and Nick wanted plenty of that. At any price? That will do nicely, Signor Berlusconi, as Fiorentina put AC Milan to shame with another combative match-winning performance.

So was Nick an evil genius or simply a player out to make the best of the athletic resources at his disposal? Think David Batty, Roy Keane and Dennis Wise. They've seen more than their share of red cards and early baths. But most fans know they'd rather have a ball-winner like any one of that lot playing for them than against them. Inelegant maybe, reckless even, but they wore their hearts on their sleeves, performed with passion, and if the odd foul meant that victory would be theirs then they knew the score. If it meant the game went pear-shaped as a result of their mis-demeanours, though, David Beckham can vouch for the unhappy consequences of such foolhardiness. Unlike Becks, poor old Nick didn't have his sarong, Posh Spice and lucrative endorsement contracts to fall back on when his stock was down in the popularity stakes.

Of course, like Beckham's Man. Utd, Fiorentina weren't exactly a poor club even in Nick's day. They could afford to splash the odd florin or two on bringing in star players from the French and Spanish leagues. The Medicis were a sort of moneybags with a liking for football, a Jack Walker or Sir John Hall of the fifteenth century. But, like the hapless Jack and Sir John, the Medicis found that, for all their millions, it wasn't so easy to buy success. They had a thirst for the power and money that was tied up in Vatican City and wanted their northern outpost to compete for Serie A and Italian Cup honours. Of course, Vatican City had their eye on higher things too, material honours at home weren't enough for them, oh no. But, having said that, the saintly figure of Peter in their side was the kind of square-ball player who gave your team the reliable platform on which domestic success could be founded.

The Medicis invested heavily in Fiorentina, trading players as the transfer bill soared. Leonardo Da Vinci was a hugely inventive player who was one of the first to sign up. He seemed to almost fly through the air, while an inscrutable

grin never left his face. A bit of a moaner some would say, but gifted all the same. Michelangelo was paired up front with Leonardo for a time, but he did have a tendency to be a tad statuesque, a polite way of saying he was immobile to the point of standing still; and when he lost an arm to young David, as he tried to carve his way through a big rock of a defence, his time was sadly up. The Medicis cast their net wider now for talent, sending the club scout, Christopher Columbus, off to track down some foreign stars. Chris reckoned he might have to go to the ends of the earth, though, as he didn't know his east from his west and he never got past

America – and we all know the Yanks aren't much cop at football. Alex Lalas or Brad Friedel anyone?

No luck on the scouting front, and all Chris's costly imports did was spice up the side, nothing more substantial than that. It was the home-grown talent of Machiavelli that really gave the Medicis' side some purpose. No more talk of transitional seasons flying in the face of the reality of mid-table mediocrity. Success was wanted this season, not in the next, or the one after that. If the team just believed in themselves then the trophies were there for the taking. Faith, that's all Nick asked of his players and directors.

Nick had a team to build. But he also knew that you don't win with just one good player, the strength of the side came from raising the level of everybody's game. He instilled order in the team too – it wasn't enough to be overflowing with ability because that could lead to laziness and the road to ruin. The game was the poorer for the woefully wasted talent of Best and Gascoigne and Nick wasn't having that happen to his players. Getting the balance right was what it was all about. He wanted to accommodate his flair players but not at the expense of the organisation of his defence. 'We can hurtle down the wings as much as we like,' Nick said as he set off on yet another of his long, mazy dribbles in the best Ginola style, 'just so long as we tackle back.' That was the sting in his authoritarian tail. George Graham would have loved old Nick to bits. And just as George preached the virtues of an impregnable back four, Nick too saw the game as won and lost at the back with his defence.

It wasn't much of a surprise that Nick's style of play was generally thought of as a bit dull, yet purposeful all the same. Hard work doesn't earn you many brownie points in the glamour stakes, however effective your attacking wing play might be in laying on balls for others to put away. With discontent mounting on the terraces, the Medicis were beginning to lose patience. Nick looked abroad once more to add a certain something to the side, but the French stars he tried to tempt with lavish wages weren't having any of it. Fast running out of ideas on how he was going to rescue Fiorentina from what was starting to look like a losing streak, Nick headed off to enter into negotiations with the one player who could outdo even him as one all too capable of putting himself about a bit – Cesare Borgia.

Starting off with Roma, Borgia was the kind of player who slaughtered defences with his piercing runs and never-say-die attitude. He'd been tempted by a move to Vatican City but contract negotiations had fallen though at the last moment, so now a move to Fiorentina held a big appeal.

But it was too late. Time had run out for Nick. While he'd been away successfully signing Borgia, the Medicis sacked him. Shaken and on the dole, Machiavelli was no longer in the thick of things. He didn't know what on earth to do with himself. Skid Via beckoned. Out on his ear, Nick tried to rebuild his career. A clown prince? He'd certainly been made a fool of, trusting those whom he'd thought of as his friends. But now it was high time to take each game as it came. Down in the nether regions of Serie B and even Serie C, he started to rule the right-wing once more. Fearless in the tackle, he dished it out with players of far-lesser talent. And if it looked like some clumsy oaf had landed Nick with an injury then he allowed himself a bit of crafty retaliation, for revenge could be sweet just so long as the ref wasn't looking. And when Nick committed such a foul you could be sure his victim would be out of the game for some time – that evened things up a bit as the season wore on.

Nick's approach to football was only occasionally spectacular, and his tricks and twists were something you savoured for their rarity value. He didn't turn on the Ginola-like style week after week so when it came it was all the more welcome. But as a team headed in freefall towards the relegation zone, the ruthless but dour stability Nick provided would nevertheless prove invaluable. And once that breathing space had been won then there was no letting up. With each precious point gained, the team would climb back to the safety of the top half and that magical forty-point target. Security, that's what Nick wanted for his team. If he had to do that all on his tod, so be it. He was too long in the tooth by now to wait on others to match his grit and courage on the pitch.

While Nick was treading water in the lower divisions,

Borgia was lording it over all and sundry in Serie A. To all intents and purposes, Borgia would have appeared to have it all. Fast, a decisive passer of the ball and, when it was needed, ruthless. He seemed to be laying the foundations for Fiorentina's long-overdue championship success, but he overstretched himself and Roma, together with Vatican City, saw off his championship challenge. A place in Europe was just about all he could now hope for.

It was Nick's chance to get back into the big time. The Medicis had never completely lost faith in him, never mind what the gossips and journos might claim. Nick would always be the man to give Fiorentina some backbone, the strength on the wing to provide the freedom for a passing game to develop in the middle of the park. And if the game turned ugly then Nick would ensure that their fightback would be fast, furious and, more to the point, win them the game. Those victories, Nick taught his players, wouldn't be down to luck either. That was only half the story; it was what they did with their boots that counted for the other half. 'You make your own luck,' was how Nick put it as he yelled at his players for one final effort. How had they managed without him, the Medicis pondered, as Nick made his way back to Fiorentina late in his career. Things could never be the same as the first time round, but at least he was back where he belonged.

Always a realist, and short on sentimentality too, Nick

knew the end of his playing career was only a few seasons away. No more Monsignor Nice Guy. His bloodied and battered opponents would no doubt retort that there'd never ever been much evidence of Monsignor Nice Guy. It was better to be feared and 3–0 up than loved and 1–0 down was how Nick judged the value of popularity. 'Sports Personality of the Year' was one award he was happy to let others win. The saintly status of Messrs Charlton, Lineker and Owen weren't for him. If players were afraid of him then he was halfway to winning the game before it had even started.

That didn't mean Nick wanted to be hated: if everyone was against him and only too eager to knock him off his pedestal then that was no good either. Getting the balance right was tricky. Often, he'd trot out the trusty old, 'you've got to be cruel to be kind', as another forward collapsed in a heap at his feet, but that didn't seem to impress the *Match of the Day* panel. Well, that's not wholly true. Alan Hansen took a shine to old Nick almost as soon as he clapped eyes on him – wonder why?

Combining a foxy way of getting the ball out of dodgy situations with brute animal strength was the mix that Machiavelli reckoned made him the composite player that no Fiorentina team could now afford to be without. Bold, most certainly never timid, he knew that bravery alone wouldn't win him any silverware but without it the team hadn't a hope in hell – one place, like his more illustrious namesake, Old Nick was never afraid of going.

The fans were happy, of course, whatever Nick's moral failings. For them it was all about results, and the virtue of a player like Machiavelli was he didn't mind how dirty he had to play as long as victory was Fiorentina's. That made for dangerous play from time to time; with his high tackles, he got booked for that offence more than most. But a yellow, or even a red card, was a small price to pay for three points won.

As the side was rebuilt around him, Nick advised the new club owner, Lorenzo de Medici, against investing too heavily this time round in foreign players. 'Mercenaries!' was how Machiavelli derided them. With no loyalty to the club's traditions, they would take their inflated wage packets stuffed full of florins and run off as soon as the going got tough. Oddly enough it's a role that his fellow Italian, Ravanelli, played to perfection down at faraway Middlesbrough four and a bit centuries later. It wasn't anything to do with nationality, of course, but buying in talent is never as good as developing your own amongst the youth and apprentice ranks. Home-grown was best then, and a team united in its purpose rather than split into too many camps was even better. Machiavelli tried to develop that unity, but it was a long time coming. The bloke who had those squashed-fly biscuits named after him, Garibaldi, was the one who would eventually pull it off and put Italy on the map. World Cup victories couldn't be far off.

At the peak of his playing career, Nick was a great hero presiding over the team that he'd built in his own fearsome image. 'The King' was what some would dub him, but Nick preferred a humbler title. A prince among players would do nicely. His purple reign seemed to stretch far into the future. But all good, and bad, things have to come to an end sometime. 1999? An eternity away when you're playing your way through the sixteenth century. And when you lose another yard of pace it's a sign of the times to hang up your boots.

Paul Cézanne

Olympique Marseille and France
Number 8 : Central Midfield

---

*'Will I reach the goal, so long sought after,
so long pursued?'*

PAUL CÉZANNE, letter to Emile Bernard,
21 September 1906

A delicate artist on the ball, Paul Cézanne would brush off defenders before gently stroking the ball across the park with a deft pass to one of his team-mates. It is no accident that for a large chunk of his career his closest pal should be Zola – Emile not Gianfranco, but novel in his approach to the game all the same.

Cézanne turned the passing game in midfield into a work of art, refusing to compromise his principles for the long ball, hoofing it up to the big lanky centre-forward up front. He saw more, much more, than a spherical object when he had a football at his feet. 'Easel! Easel!' His most fervent supporters would chant as he sketched out more than twenty passes in the middle third of the pitch, pulling opponents out of position as the ball made its way relentlessly towards its final destiny, the back of the net. As the results went his way, it was no time before Paul was making an impression, even if he did have a tendency to hit the post too often for some of his fans' liking.

His form never left him, though sometimes he would be left in the shadows of more glamorous stars grabbing the limelight as they toe-poked home the ball that Paul had delivered to their feet. Paul wanted to be in the frame too, why should others grab all the glory?

Canvassing opinion, he asked Victor Hugo's advice, but he seemed even more miserable with his lot than Paul, so no luck there. Paul tried his hand instead at breaking forward more, keeping possession, but still life let him down. Claude Monet joined Paul in midfield for a few seasons, a past master but still quick enough. His shimmering runs in the bright Marseille sunshine would dazzle and delight as he made his way across the playing surface. And it wasn't long before they were queuing round the block to see his work. Like Paul his touch was light, but devastating all the same, and at long last Paul began to believe that he did belong in this team. Paul was slowly learning that playing football wasn't just about keeping your own form but staying in line too, position was all if you were to catch the other lot offside. Arm in the air as yet another linesman's flag went up, years later Tony Adams would learn to appreciate that there wasn't much you had to teach a Frenchman about the Highbury way.

Sitting high in the stands, fans could see the tidy patterns of the passing game Cézanne was painting. He added colour to the team with his occasionally fiery outbursts, all impetuous and self-righteous, but as long as he escaped with only a yellow card the supporters forgave him. But a red card, that was the sign of the long, lonely walk to the dressing-room. Down to ten men, Marseille would be lucky to escape a pasting.

A colourful character, Paul wasn't one to settle for a draw. He wanted a victory, and was happy to work long and hard for those vital three points. Playing to the gallery would earn him more than a few friends along the way, but he'd put up with the critics too just so long as he finished on the winning side.

Paul was a realist when it came to what his club could expect to achieve. They were short on players of genuine class, but from the ordinary squad around him, Paul reckoned he'd make something a bit special. They might create a scene with their petulant displays of diving and off-the-ball incidents – the team was stuffed full with Latin temperament after all – but this lot would work their socks off too. *Sans Culottes* – well, almost. The players would give their all, and there was no more that Paul could ask of them. He wasn't one for grand symbolic gestures, the work rate of his fellow players was what really mattered to him.

But Paul could be innovative too. Work rate was just the platform on which all the fancy stuff depended for the final result. He remained an outsider, drawing up a plan on his pre-match blackboard of how he would like to see the team play, but unsure of whether it would all be an illusion by the time kick-off came around. The team would never be built around a fellow like Cézanne; whatever the scale of his exceptional talent he remained too much of an individualist. The contrast with the rest of the team was obvious for all to see as a picture of this most artistic of players began to take shape.

Paul had a great eye for the ball. Conjuring up opportunities out of nothing, he was in his element on the edge of the box covering more ground than the rest of the midfield put together. Even the most level-headed of observers would be tempted to lose all sense of perspective as Paul delivered the ball from seemingly impossible angles out on the far touchline. A diagonal cross across the pitch would cut the opposition's defence in two, they just didn't know which way to turn, and in that moment of indecision a goal would be Paul's for the taking. But not always, unfortunately, since he was a fussy player, never quite satisfied to simply rush into the box. Adding more and more detail to the patient build-up, the time this would take sometimes allowed the defenders to regroup and pack the penalty area to keep the ball out long enough to defeat Paul's determined goalbound efforts.

The team needed a big hitter, a predator up front who'd snatch those chances and put them away in one glorious instant. Vincent Van Gogh, a big-money transfer from Holland, seemed to be the target man the club had been waiting for. But he failed the medical, the bandages rather gave him away, and with only one ear it didn't matter how loud the bench bellowed at him, he'd never hear their instructions. So the Cézanne style, at least for the moment, remained intact. In fact the bright lights of all this fame and fortune were beginning to suit Paul, his formation was beginning to become the natural way for Marseille to play and he was certainly back in favour, with or without Van Gogh at his side.

As his career developed, Paul's pace certainly slowed down, but at the same time he was learning to organise himself with a rigorous discipline that kept him out of trouble. The combination would help him to play well into his thirties. He was now beginning to determine more carefully the nature of his object, the goal. While his play might be less colourful as the seasons went by, he more than made up for this by doing nothing simply for effect. Stripped down to the basics, his style was simple and easy enough to watch. Calm and heroic with his foot on the ball, Paul would ask his players to line up behind him. Layer after layer of Marseille shirts would roll forward, short passes between them meaning they kept control of the ball. The compact formation meant that, as they entered the final third, longer passes were possible, broken up with the occasional short ones. In line, they'd pass the ball to one another and thus the team made their mark as nobody's pushover.

But still Paul wasn't satisfied. The composition of the team was all wrong, it lacked balance. The shape was bold enough, but it just didn't look right. Not yet anyway. It was back to the drawing-board once again. Paul would structure the team around the natural talents at their disposal, and he did this in such a way that the lads would find something in themselves that they'd never seen before. The one-dimensional back four was no more, for starters. Playing in a line was simply not enough. Bursting forward, passing and tackling, work rate and flair, strong in the air yet confident on the ground, Paul wanted an all-round contribution from his defenders. They had to create their own space out on the pitch, not just rely on what had previously been fixed positions and roles. This would give the team the depth that Paul had hankered after for so long. Overlapping, he'd not only have four defenders, but a back four who could launch attacks from deep in their own half too. The lives of his defenders were no longer still, they weren't motionless figures but alive to the opportunities their movement could provide for the rest of the team.

The way Cézanne now had his side playing seemed all back to front. The full-backs would launch attacks with their darting runs while the forwards acted as the first line of defence and the opposition were thrown off-balance. While there was a danger, as always, of the fans getting things out of proportion, Marseille did seem to be on the way back at last.

Paul didn't want to shatter his supporters' illusions, but he

did stress constantly that the secret of his success was keeping things basic. It was all down to how he arranged his plain-and-simple players. This is what would decide whether the club figured in the top three or not. But as the season drew to an end, Paul did allow the players to experiment. The square ball was introduced, boxed in by this new cube formation that Paul's new signing, Pablo Picasso, helped pioneer – their opponents were forced back on to the defensive and the goals mounted up. Paul was less sure, though, when the American international, Jackson Pollock, joined them and started spraying the ball all around the pitch. Paul was all for innovation, but things could be taken too far. When the youthful Damien Hirst suggested he had a way to give any side a right stuffing, Paul knew it was time to get back to his beloved basics.

The trouble with these new talents now being attracted to the side was that they played the game with too much emotion. Paul preferred composition as the way to find and make space – let the raw talent come through, but give the players a stable base on which they could shine. His players were expected to have a powerful and immediate presence, at the back or up front, and this would help them to keep calm when the results went against them – as they inevitably would someday. It was the interaction between these different elements in the side that would help them to see their way clear to the objective reality of their final league placing.

As the run-in approached, Paul dropped an absolute bombshell that would shake the traditionalists in the club to the core. Olympique Marseille had always played in white with just a touch of blue. But Paul wanted to change all this, he wanted shirts full of colour. Reds, yellows, greens, browns even, splashed all over so he could pick out his players against both the pitch and the backdrop of the stands. Mad? Well, Alex Ferguson would use the same excuse when the umpteenth Man. Utd away-strip change of the season had given him a side kitted out in grey. 'The wrong coloured shirts,' was his retort when asked to explain the team's defeat to lowly Southampton. And the modern Dutch master of the game, Ruud Gullit, changed Newcastle's socks to white so it would be easier for his players to spot each other for passes to feet. Fat lot of good that wheeze proved to be. Paul would have preferred a bolder use of colour to break up the monochrome look of the Geordie Toon Army, but when Ruud tried to add a dash of silver he didn't have much luck, and was soon enough on his way.

Paul wasn't one for club history, so it was out with the classic Marseille white strip and in with the multicoloured look that he now favoured. But if it did the trick who'd be complaining then? The effect, luckily enough, was immediate. No more melting into the background, the player's figures were caught in bold outline as they rushed up the pitch. In open play nobody could miss them, there was nothing transparent about this lot as they put the title beyond everybody else's reach. The whole composition of the side, colours and all, was settled at last. And when he went up to pick up the championship trophy Paul was happy to take the acclaim at last. 'What a picture.' He shyly replied: 'Well, you would say that.' A humble rustic type to the last.

Homer

Blyth Spartans and Ancient Greece
Number 9 : Centre-forward

'Nothing makes a man so famous during his lifetime as what he can achieve with his hands and feet.'

HOMER, *The Odyssey*

HOMERE POETE GREC.
Chap. 20.

There is no arguing with Homer's selection; a Greek bearing gifts is what you need in any ambitious team. And when the gift is the guarantee of thirty goals a season, then the Spartans' title ambitions were halfway to being sorted. Not exactly a saint, Homer could mix it with the worst of them, but if it's an explanation of how to put the ball in the back of the net you're looking for, he's your man.

With Pythagoras playing in the hole just behind him, Homer was able to build on the neat triangles that his fellow Greek sketched out across the park as the ball crossed left to right, back again then down the pitch to his own defence before moving unerringly up to the centre circle. From here Socrates would carry the ball forward, asking questions of the most resistant of defences. Finding himself isolated and surrounded by the other lot's pair of strapping central defenders, Socrates would invariably strive on alone, finding his own way to goal. Out on the edge of the box, Homer waited in vain as Socrates' final touch let them both down, time and time again. Poor service is the downfall of even the most gifted of strikers, so Socrates was banished to see out his career making up the numbers with the youth team. But even here his inept forward runs were a bad influence on the group of talented youngsters that had just been poached from under the noses of the Spartan's big rivals, Athens. A sorry future lay ahead for Socrates and no one was exactly surprised when his favourite tipple, Hemlock Sunrise on the rocks, pushed him over the edge and out of the reckoning for ever.

Plato was the new kid on the Acropolis whom the board bought in to stiffen up Homer's attacking midfield options. A real guv'nor in the traditional Paul Ince mould, he didn't believe in cosy team talks or any of that namby-pamby interpersonal stuff. 'Get stuck in and win the ball' was more Plato's style. He fitted into the Spartans line-up immediately, ruthless and ready to lay siege to the opposition's penalty box. Give him the soft-centred Athenians anytime and he'd show them a physical thing or two. Ruling the pitch, Plato was absolutely convinced of his natural-born talent to win, and woe betide anyone who doubted him. In the slot that Socrates had now vacated, Plato acted as Homer's guardian of the midfield, weighing up the options as he dictated the pace of the game to Homer's liking. And just so long as nobody questioned his 5–4–1 system, everything for the Spartans would be hunky-dory. The promised land of league titles and lifting the cup surely couldn't be that far off.

But the trouble with Plato was that he had this habit of rubbing his team-mates up the wrong way. Harsh discipline and tough tackling was all well and good, but you had to let people play a bit too. And with those titles and cups seeming as much in the distance as ever, Plato began to fall out of favour. In his place, Homer paired up with Aristotle, a bloke who had this uncanny knack of knitting together a bunch of individuals into a team. His greatest finding was Alexander, a player who, when the defence was tied up in knots, was the first to battle the ball out of the heap of tangled bodies before giving his hard-pressed defenders breathing space. Aristotle was soon an essential member of the team, honing skilled marksmen out of the workaday fellows that had previously just made up the numbers. He wanted to make them into party animals, full of the joys of life as they marched out on to the pitch, heads held high, a beating breast and a big grin on their faces. 'Think of yourselves as winners, and you'll *be* winners,' Aristotle urged his team-mates. And pleased enough with a home draw, their modest ambitions did lead to a certain sense of contented achievement, even if they weren't actually winning yet.

Aristotle was a stickler for the rule book too. Cautions, yellow cards and early baths weren't for his team. Archimedes might disagree about the latter, but then all he did was ship too much water on an already sodden pitch. 'Eureka!' – well, only if his craftily devised postponement meant a result later in the season. No, Aristotle wanted his players to play to the spirit of the game, not just because the ref insisted on it, but because it was right. If no other trophy came their way, at least they'd be dead certs for the end-of-season fair-play award.

And thereby hangs Homer's tale. Come the end of the season the trophy cabinet was still bare – not even that fair-play award to show for all their efforts. Crestfallen, Homer was feeling like the *Iliad* done bad. It was time to put one over some big-name foreign opponents, and they don't come any bigger than Troy. A make-or-break season, if they couldn't beat the Trojans then it really would be time for Homer to hang up his sandals.

Troy had been the bane of the Spartans' lives for some time now. The bad blood between them was down to their top man, Paris, stealing away Helen, the beautiful wife of the Spartans' captain. A face that could launch a thousand boats, no wonder the cockney Greeks, forerunners of those other glory hunters, the cockney Reds, dubbed her 'boat race'. Now the prospect of putting one over those Trojan pretty-boys led to an even bigger increase in the Spartans' travelling support, with fans signing up from far and wide for this great overseas adventure. As they put out to sea, the cheer went up: 'We sing when we're rowing, We only sing when we're rowing,' over and over the Aegean.

Homer now found a new ally for himself up front. No

more of this playing deep, he needed a player who would take the game to the other lot, and in Agamemnon the Spartans had just that. But after the first match ended in an away win for the Spartans, 'Aga' (as he was inevitably known after the fans had got themselves in all sorts of alphabetical trouble on the terraces with 'give us an A, give us a G . . .) fell out with the undoubted star of the side, Achilles. It was all down to who got the biggest slice of the win bonus, not to mention what the un-PC Aga referred to as the 'totty'. Achilles couldn't believe it: he'd made the chances, sent in the crosses, ploughed his way past tackle after tackle but he wasn't going to get what he reckoned was his fair share of the spoils.

All bitter and twisted, Achilles refused to play ball. The team would have to get by without him as he went into the biggest sulk the ancient world had ever seen. The lads tried everything to persuade him to change his mind, but he was having none of it. He was a well-connected little blighter too, getting his mum to call in some favours with Zeus – who before Rupert Murdoch was even thought of, had The Sun in the palm of his hand, not to mention The Times and Sky too. Thunderbolts and lightning, darkened heavens, the odd earthquake, old man Zeus played merry hell with the playing conditions as the Spartans sank to defeat.

Achilles had a heart though, even if his tendons were a bit on the sore side. His best mate, Patroclus, asked if he could borrow his boots to try and give the side some sort of luck and Achilles relented. 'Patto' blazed through the Trojan defences for a while, but boots alone don't make the man and in front of goal he died a death. Achilles was, by now, and quite rightly, beside himself with guilt. His once-winning side had sunk this low, and all because of his own stupid pride. He knew there was only one thing for it – he had to get back out on the pitch before all was lost.

With all these defeats to avenge, Achilles was in a foul mood. His career had been cut short by seasons of inactivity but now he was ready to make up for all that. The glory days, and nights – if Zeus could help out with the odd full moon to light up the pitch – would be here again. Of course, he could have chosen the easy life, toiling away season after season in quiet anonymity, but that wasn't his style. Achilles wanted to be the hero of his side, not just some also-ran.

He knew it wouldn't last – the good times never do. His heel was causing him loads of grief – maybe this was the career-threatening injury he'd always feared. Bandaged up, he played on until, with the last kick of what proved to be his final match, he buried the ball in the back of his bitter rival Hector's net. That heel would wait no longer, the operating table beckoned as Achilles bade farewell to the pitch one final time.

For Homer though, the game was far from over. The Trojans might be done and dusted as, by the end, the Spartans had driven a coach and horses through their wooden defence, but there was the long trip home still to face. And, no doubt, there would be the odd score to settle *en route*, too.

Odysseus was the man to lead Homer's side back home to Greece. Shame then that he couldn't find his way out of a piece of pitta bread. All over the Mediterranean he took the team on a boat trip from hell or, as they called it in those days, Hades. Playing into the wind, they even lost out to a one-eyed side who should have been a right pushover. The Cyclops were nothing, though, compared to Blue Circe FC who soon reduced the Spartans to swine, foraging for the ball as they forgot all they once knew about the art of winning. Next they were in mortal danger of being eaten alive by some fine young cannibals who were just a tad on the big side. Odysseus had to dig deep to get his lads out of what proved to be one more near-defeat. But he proved adept at just this kind of rescue mission, turning the game on its head as the point was won. And there was no finer moment than when he tied himself to his near post while the siren calls urged him upfield. Putting that boot out, legs all askance, he saved the ball from crossing the line, Odysseus lived to fight another day.

But, unlike Achilles, Odysseus didn't have Zeus in the palm of his hand. He had been warned from on high not to sacrifice the big oafs who made up his central-defence pairing if he wanted to see his side safe though to their journey's end. If that was what the man from Mount Olympus wanted then

Odysseus was happy enough to go along with it. After all, you break up your tried and trusted defence at your peril, just ask that nice Monsieur Wenger. Unfortunately, it only took Odysseus to take his eye off the ball for a moment and the rest of the side had stitched up a deal to offload what was a bit of a cumbersome twosome to all intents and purposes. Odysseus was ruined because, before you could say 'Feta cheese sandwich and plenty of oil,' Zeus had let fly with the thunderbolts. Odysseus' dreams of getting the team back home in one piece were wrecked. He was all washed up. And yet the strangest things can happen at sea. Of all the beaches in the world his son chose to wander along, lonely as a cloud,

it was the one Odysseus found himself on. And we're talking Ithaca, which is miles away from Casablanca, so there.

Father and son double-acts don't always work out, but this one was made in heaven, or should that be Olympus? Odysseus's old lady, Penelope, was in danger of losing her Elgin marbles if she couldn't find a way of keeping all her lecherous admirers away. She'd managed to convince them they were on a promise if they'd just let her finish her beloved tapestry. Centuries before the invention of Anadin, this proved to be the longest 'I've got a headache' in ancient history, as each night she carefully unpicked all the knitting and stitching she'd done during the day. 'Not tonight, Big Urn,' for the BC crowd.

But Odysseus and his son Telemachus knew she wouldn't be able to keep this up for ever. Down on his luck and clean out of Armani tunics, Odysseus wrapped some rags around his shoulders and made his way to his old home. So near, yet so far, he'd been away for so long he wasn't sure Penelope would have him back. After all, ten years is one almighty away trip, not even the M1 would hold you up for that long, cones and all.

Penelope, meanwhile, was at the end of her tether. There was no obvious sign of Odysseus returning and the attentions of her admirers were getting ever more pressing. So she set a test, one she was sure nobody would be able to pass and that might just buy her some more time. Odysseus had been the kind of banana-kick specialist that makes David Beckham look like a wet Saturday in Hartlepool as he bent the ball round another line of defenders, so a trial of footballing skills seemed the ideal set-up.

Delicately, Penelope placed the ball and asked each of her admirers to bend it round a series of strategically positioned cut-out figures that bore an uncanny resemblance to the immobile figure of Tony Adams. With one arm in the air, these statues were nigh on impossible to miss and, barring a lucky deflection, avoiding contact with them was the one sure way to goal. Each of the lecherous types tried in turn, cursing themselves as they failed. They had neither the strength nor the top spin to succeed. Then up stepped Homer's old mate, Odysseus, though of course no one recognised him in his rags and unsightly facial hair. He unleashed his coiled left leg with a ferocity that left a 'whoosh' hanging in the air. The ball spun off his foot, bending first to the left before curling off to the right. The statues were left standing, the back of the net beckoned. There was so much forward momentum in that kick that it was almost as if the ball would never stop, but it did. Right in the back of the net. And Odysseus, for now of course everyone knew who he was, lived happily ever after with his beloved Penelope. It's all Greek to me, sighed a passing muse, giving Homer, still cowering behind a delphic column, an idea for what proved to be a best-selling epic of love, death and football.

Jean-Paul Sartre

Paris Saint-Germain and France
Number 10 : Inside-left

'*In a football match, everything is complicated by the presence of the opposite team.*'

JEAN-PAUL SARTRE, *Critique of Dialectical Reason*, Volume One

Long before Patrick Vieira and his fellow Frenchman Emmanuel Petit became the exiled heroes of Arsenal's North Bank, Jean-Paul Sartre was provoking the '*Sacre Bleus*!' in the cafés and bars of the Paris Left Bank.

Not much of a one for bri-nylon multiweaves – all that static could play havoc with his scraped back and gelled down hairstyle – Jean-Paul was an early champion of hand-knitted polo neck jumpers, preferably black, although the pedantic refs he came across weren't too keen on the colour clash with their own uniform of authority. 'Who's Les Bastards in the black?' the Paris Saint-Germain wags on the Parc de Princes terraces would shout out fresh from their half-time croissants and cafés au lait. The sophisticated diet clearly didn't do any wonders for the PSG fans' natural-born liking for an expletive. Ref and Jean-Paul would look at each other. 'Do they mean me?' they'd ask in unison. And so began Jean-Paul's long search for his inner self.

While he played up front and on the left, Sartre always

contributed more than his fair share to the defensive duties. He tackled back with speed and efficiency, a trait that all too easily goes unrecognised amidst all the Gallic charm of the likes of Ginola and Zidane. But just ask your Andy Grays and Alan Hansens to tot up the tackles made by these lads in their post-match summaries and you'll see that David, Zinedine and the rest serve their team-mates well.

Jean-Paul wanted to put the ball in the back of the net, sure enough. But the being and nothingness of a clean sheet remained his ultimate goal. A hat-trick brought him pleasure, but if that meant throwing players forward leaving the back four exposed and scraping home to a 3–2 win he left the field full of melancholy. Berating his fellow forwards to push up and act as the first line of defence, Jean-Paul could cut a fearsome figure. All of five foot and three inches, he had the makings of a Nobby Stiles or Billy Bremner within that tidy frame of his as he puffed out his chest and gave of his best. '*Merde*!' he exclaimed as another soft goal was given away. All this *laissez-faire* was getting them nowhere.

Simone de Beauvoir was his unconventional choice of a playing partner, though she was never, ever satisfied with being just Jean-Paul's number two. Simone expected to play as an equal, or not at all, and whilst they both took their turns at playing alone, and away, the pairing did last.

To his fans, Jean-Paul was nothing less than a pheno-menon, though he himself was never fully happy with the label. He wasn't so humble as to deny that he brought something special, unique even, to the team, but he felt that, given time, any player could make a contribution that would come to be regarded as something special too. His ability wasn't God-given, Jean-Paul was sure of that. It was all down to self-belief and the will to succeed, qualities that are somewhere deep within ourselves and that we all have.

The team had a tendency to play the ball down the left, where Jean-Paul was positioned for most of his career, rather than down the right. Jean-Paul had no problem with that, he liked to get the service after all, what forward wouldn't? But he got all bitter and twisted when the tactics became predictable, too easy for others to read, formulaic even. The 1967–68 season was his happiest time, as an injection of fresh young players shook things up. The play was still down the left, but these new lads would storm out of the defence at great speed, playing much further out on the left than Jean-Paul had been used to. And the Chinese import that they now welcomed into the squad, Mao Tse-tung, even advocated a long march into the opposition's penalty area to break down the great wall of a defence the opposition had set up. Things were really starting to open out, but when they came up against a crack Soviet side, they suffered their first set-back. Jean-Paul became less sure of his position on the inside-left and joined the youngsters breaking into the team in playing far out wide on the left. The tactic worked for a while, but

Mao was getting sent off so often for his ferocious guarding of the ball that he'd collected enough cards to make a little red book out of them. The suspensions were hitting the squad hard, so Jean-Paul looked to other imports to strengthen the squad. His liking for Algerians didn't go down too well with some of his domestic critics and they put up a front, but Jean-Paul was having none of this. More and more imported stars started to arrive, and Jean-Paul welcomed them with open arms. Kafka was given a trial, though Nietzsche was rejected because of his poor disciplinary record – beyond good and evil isn't going to go down very well with the likes of David Elleray, is it? Dostoevsky impressed for a while, but in the end had to go as he was a bit of an idiot, though the brothers Karamazov he brought with him stayed around. They were thought of as a touch on the classic side by some.

Stuffed full with international stars of this quality, Sartre's team surely had it made. But Jean-Paul was yet to be convinced. He was all for strengthening the squad, and a touch of glamour wouldn't go amiss either. But all alone out on the pitch, he felt abandoned to the fate of the game while at the same time free to do as he liked so long as he scored. The conflict of contradictions was pulling him this way and that – he was only human after all. The responsibility of getting the team back on a winning track weighed heavily on Jean-Paul's shoulders. He didn't want to be a miserable old so-and-so but what was the alternative if they didn't start scoring?

Jean-Paul looked to his costly imports to come up with some answers. The Austrian star Sigmund Freud was laid out cold, unconscious in the dressing-room. He seemed happy enough, but what use he'd be in that state nobody seemed to know. The left-winger they'd just brought in from Germany, Karl Marx, only seemed to be interested in the means of producing goals, what went on in the super-structure of the defence was no concern of his. Jean-Paul was getting nowhere fast with those two. He knew some thought the problem was his ego, but that was just unfair. He wasn't going to sell himself short, but what he wanted to do was raise the level of the entire side. If the players just became more conscious of the game going on around them then that would be a start; they could begin concentrating on the contribution each of them could make to a successful side.

Jean-Paul was loyal enough to his older players. They'd seen him though the lean times, but all this thinking was cramping René Descartes' style. His presence on the pitch just wasn't enough any more. And the essence of Socrates' play, good as it might once have been, didn't justify his existence in the side any more, either.

Having found themselves, Jean-Paul's new-look team would start to understand that just about anything was possible. The prospect filled them with anguish: they might as easily be looking at the big drop into the second division as the glory of a championship or a cup. 'All to play for,' was what Jean-Paul would offer them as the start of the season beckoned. Jean-Paul just loved the thrill of being there as the first game began: he knew well enough that the campaign would be a long haul, but at least they were in with as much of a chance as anyone.

The squad had plenty of depth, and as for those who could only get a seat on the bench, Jean-Paul patiently explained to them that nobody was superfluous. He had to prepare for every contingency so their time would surely come as the season unfolded and cup runs lengthened.

And if the results did go against them then Jean-Paul would laugh and joke with the lads after the game. No more of his melancholy, he preferred to just wisecrack at the absurdity of what he surely wouldn't be the last to dub a 'funny old game'. But a 3–0 home defeat at the hands of their south-coast rivals, Olympique Marseille, did push to the limit the Paris Saint-Germain faithful's ability to find meaning in a meaningless world. Reality was one thing, but a relegation scrap really wasn't much to look forward to. Jean-Paul knew it was time to start asking some questions of a side that he felt was blessed with too many unfulfilled talents. He needed to make some demands of them, and if they responded positively then he knew that at the end of the season they'd still be up there with the top flight of French football. But if the lads wouldn't respond then no team was too good to go down into the black hole of the lower divisions, as Nottingham Forest discovered to their cost more than once.

Jean-Paul would have been the last to decry the value of his star players to the side. But they were stars because of all the players who performed a role in the background too. The defenders were the ones most likely to be in the shadows of the glitz and the glamour of the goal-of-the-season types up front. The midfield ball-winners and play-makers occupied the space somewhere in between stardom and anonymity, but take any element out of the formation and they'd all just be a bunch of nobodies. It was the mix of talents that made Jean-Paul's side so unpredictable. But no team could be sure of success and any that did think they had some divine right to

fill a top-three position, season after season, would soon enough come crashing down with a bump. The once mighty Everton, anybody?

Sartre's problem was that Paris Saint-Germain had such an awe-inspiring history of success that any current side was expected to live up to it, or else. But Jean-Paul appreciated there was nothing he could do about the past; it was the present that he was concerned with. If he could turn things around this season, and the team lifted a trophy, then they'd be making history themselves, never mind what the players of yesteryear had done.

Of course, until the results started to go in their favour there were plenty who would moan on about a side that was failing to live up to its potential once again. Jean-Paul put it all down to bad faith, a failure to believe in what eleven individuals could do. He sincerely believed in himself, and all he asked of the fans and the players was that they should believe in themselves too.

Jean-Paul wasn't one for sticking with the same side, match after match. So he surprised many by changing his forward line around the time the club started what looked like that long-awaited winning streak. But it was his choice, and his alone. What Jean-Paul was preparing himself for was the other side – each team posed him a different challenge, and to win he had to be ready for every eventuality. A pacy wing-back demanded that Jean-Paul cut inside more often and play down the middle of the park directly behind his centre-forward. But if the other lot boasted a tough-tackling but cumbersome full-back, Jean-Paul would prefer to go wide and use the extra yard that he thought he'd have on his opponent to put in some crosses from the byline.

As Paris Saint-Germain climbed the table, they fell under everybody's gaze. They found themselves in the spotlight and judgements were being made on their ability to maintain their run. If they faltered, the players knew they'd only have themselves to blame and the shame of failure would be with them for ever. At least they were up for the challenge, and the pride they all shared they were sure would see them through the odd set-back on the way to the league championship. After all, looked at objectively, a point dropped, even three, isn't the disaster it first appears if the rest of the results go in your favour.

The players, Jean-Paul told them, could only be certain of one thing and that was they were free agents and never mind what Eric Hall might tell them. Out on the pitch nobody could help them but themselves. And, as they came to believe in their own ability, the winning streak started to really gather some momentum. The team had an air of responsibility about them, they were making their mark and the glory days seemed, at last, to be on the way back. And if they failed to lift the league championship by the end of the season, the lads knew that this time there could be no excuses.

The desire to win was infectious, but the passion to be someone was even more irresistible. Jean-Paul told the players that each one of them was unique, but the secret lay with playing the game in such a way that brought the best out of all of them, not just out of the one star striker.

Jean-Paul never lost sight of the contribution that each and every player was making. It was through their collective effort that a trophy would eventually be theirs. As the long season drew to a close, the lads knew it was the way they had held together as a team when seemingly everything was going against them that had seen them through to their championship victory. As the final whistle was blown and the team knew the title was theirs, Jean-Paul came over all misty-eyed and dizzy. 'Sick as a parrot?' one of his team-mates asked.

'No, just nausea,' Jean-Paul answered. He'd been searching for a method that would bring his beloved PSG some long sought-after success for ages, and now he had a reason to celebrate, not critique. Things would never be the same again – well, not till next season in any case.

Jacques Derrida

Paris Saint-Germain and France
Number 11: Outside-left

'There is nothing beyond the touchline.'

JACQUES DERRIDA, in *Society Matters*,
Autumn–Winter 1998

A huge influence on the pitch, Jacques Derrida was one of those wide players who could play down either the left or the right wing and, as a bit of a drifter, had a perplexing habit to play down both in the course of a single game. He undermined the gaffer's tactical master plan and match-winning concepts with his free-floating creative play in the channels, but if his crosses hit home then who's complaining?

The natural inclination of most football managers is to have a particular team formation that he expects his players to stick to through the fifty or so games of an average season's league and cup campaign. Four-four-two or maybe just three at the back and pack the midfield with five, or there's the Christmas tree with the lone striker up front. Each manager has his own favourite way to position his team, and whatever the club or set of players he's lumbered with, this becomes his trademark way of winning, or losing. Jacques wasn't having any of this. The rigour of fixed positions, each player with a particular part of the pitch to patrol, wasn't his way of playing at all. He wanted the freedom to roam, pick up loose balls, pop up where you'd least expect him and, with a twist of his hips and a flick of his deadly left foot, shake things up a bit.

The fans loved him for it, while the bench just screamed at the wayward star as their carefully laid plans went to pot. For all that flair, you could never be certain whether Jacques' wing play was working for you or against you. But what no one could deny, though plenty tried, was that Derrida was a careful reader of the game. Maybe he wasn't a textbook winger in the mould of Sir Stanley Matthews, George Best or fellow-countryman David Ginola, but he knew all the moves right enough: hurtling down the wing one moment, changing direction, losing his marker then rifling in a cross to the centre-forward flying through the air to meet it with his head. And when the move didn't quite come off, Derrida would descend into the foulest of moods. His deep Gallic brogue became completely impenetrable to even his closest team-mates, and, muttering obscure obscenities of desire under his breath, he'd find himself booked for dissent by refs who weren't used to all this answering back.

In trouble with the game's authorities, Derrida never-theless knew that a sending-off would do him and his team no good at all. He learnt to curb his tongue well before he might find himself trudging towards the touchline and the ignominy of an early bath. Instead, he started querying in his own mind the lines of attack he was pursuing down the wings. How were all these defenders stopping him in his fast-moving tracks? Did he need to cut inside or was the answer to draw more of the other lot's back four out wide to free up the space in the centre? Martin Heidegger down the right wing seemed to have it licked for a while, his crosses were full of authority and reached their target time and again, but as defences started to push him further and further right he completely lost it and ended up on that list of players who never fulfilled their early potential. In his place, new signing Roland Barthes proved to be a far better bet and helped Derrida greatly in finding the place where his crosses should land.

Jacques was grateful for all the assistance he could get, but whatever the advice Roland and others like him proffered, he wasn't going to stick to any fixed position for the full ninety minutes. This made it impossible for the likes of Hansen, Brooking and Lawrenson to summarise precisely what Derrida's contribution to the game had been. Inevitably he would have played a blinder, pulling defenders out of position as they tried to counter his runs, but what exactly had he done? Like the defenders before them, the commentators simply couldn't pin Derrida down.

Most goals had a simple enough beginning, middle and end. Build from the back, hold the ball in midfield, release it to the forwards and before you know it the ball's in the back of the net. With Derrida in the side, all such simplicities were history, and this was what made it so difficult for anyone to make their mind up about him. For every flash of brilliance there was a spectacularly wasted opportunity, and shifting the balance from the negatives to the positives would try the patience of even the most dedicated of coaches.

Derrida would traditionally kick off out on either wing, left or right, the choice didn't matter as much to him as some other players. With two good feet, he would trouble the other team's full-backs either way. His special magic, though, wasn't his wing play – there were plenty of others better than him on the right or the left. It was when he slipped across the pitch, leaping over the deadly sliding tackles of his op-ponents, that he had the defence unravelled and the goals would start to pile up. A slippery customer, sly even, he was one of the first players who floated around filling the hole behind the front two while signifying his contribution with goals of his own and assists for others.

Some die-hard traditionalists remained ambivalent. Derrida wasn't what you'd call a team-player. There was no easy way he could convince his critics, though: the game Jacques played was always unstable, fraught with risk and, if less gifted players tried to follow his way, they'd certainly come unstuck. A favourite with the supporters, he was, none-theless, never all that popular in the changing-room. His name on the team sheet meant the rest of the side had to kiss goodbye to the solid foundations that for more seasons than most of them cared to remember had at least given them the security of mid-table mediocrity.

Before Derrida had come along, the Swiss international, Saussure, had talked a good game. Jacques Lacan was a psycho in the middle of the park whose analysis was faultless. Louis Althusser gave the team a sense of how things would fall into place once he'd sorted out the left side, while Claude Levi-Strauss was the source of some great team spirit, with his talk of kith and kin, though if you ribbed Claude about his denim cut-downs held together with copper rivets he went crazy, saying they might be his genes but he blamed an impostor from across the Atlantic with whom he would forever be confused.

With this lot playing for them, the club's place in the middle of the table was secure enough. There was a sense of structure, and while the idea of actually winning anything was hardly ever present, at least they'd seen off the threat of relegation.

But for Derrida all this talk of merely surviving in the top flight was neither here nor there. To have at least a sniff of the title might mean the occasional flirting with relegation. It was better to risk all than to suffer the boredom of risking nothing. Between presence and absence was how Derrida not only liked to play his game, but also how he wanted the entire club to think of football. If he was at his best floating in and out of the game then the same would be true of the team, rising to the highs of the top of the table one moment then a few defeats later sinking to the lows of being rooted at the bottom.

A rollercoaster of a season beckoned with Derrida now at the helm. He brought in new players. He put nobody at the centre of his team, dispersed the ball to all four corners of the pitch and if he was ever-present he was also never quite all there out on the pitch either. Confusion ruled, but with the results going Derrida's way nobody was any the wiser.

He was now playing both outside- and inside-left. He was at the heart of everything, undoing all the expectations that others had of him. He never doubted that he could do it all on his own, though he also knew he performed best with the team gathered around him. Most of all, he knew he needed some decent opposition to force the team to raise their game. And as they did, he began to calmly deconstruct the defences that had been so carefully put together to play him and his side off the park.

Running first to the left then to the right, the other side's defenders were pulled all out of position. Unable to work out whether to go with him or let others take him on, they were left full of indecision. Next, Derrida would turn and go up the middle of the pitch, the opposition's midfield now all around him before they even realised they'd been fooled. He'd cleared a path for others to go wide, there was now loads of space on the wings, and his inside-forwards moved out ready for the ball to come their way. The reversal of roles worked a treat. The ball was released from Derrida's feet and he moved like lightning down the centre of the field – the one place no one ever expected to find him. The switch of position didn't worry Jacques, though, and with the ball whistling in, all he had to do was climb high in the air and nod the ball home.

It was Derrida's name on the score sheet, but he knew it wasn't all down to him. It was the team that had made his goal possible. But by the time the next game came around, Derrida would have shifted things around once again. He was a big believer in rotation, not letting his players settle into a routine. Nobody could be sure of their place, the moves that he favoured demanding different formations on a week-to-week basis.

Immanuel Kant was one player who wasn't convinced by Derrida's constant changing of a winning side. He liked his game pure, believing there was a reason why some players were winners and others losers. His game was built on a rigid line between his outside-lefts and rights, who crossed the ball, and his inside players who would shoot or head it home. But Derrida was having none of that. He was all for his players going down the blind side and each and every one of them had to be confident on the ball, full of the art of the dribble whether they were destined to defend or attack. In

Jacques' team the numbers the players wore on their backs would lose all sense of meaning.

With confusion likely to reign on the pitch, Derrida's sides didn't make for comfortable viewing. He raged against systems – all he wanted was the ball to be played across the surface. Keeping it low and tight was how Jacques liked his team to play. Rousseau figured for a while in Derrida's line-up. A natural midfielder, he played a civilised kind of game, elegant and cultured, but he would keep going on about how the side had to react to the way their opponents played. This saw him fall out with Derrida, who wanted his team to revolve around their own sense of difference, not the strictures opponents imposed on them.

Skimming across the surface, the ball traced its uncertain way towards the goal. Of course, there was nothing original about any of this, Derrida was honest enough to admit that plenty had gone where he was taking his team before. But it was the possibility of success that marked Derrida out from the rest. He knew that he had to win some space in front of goal, for here half-chances might just make it into the back of the net. Talking a good game was all well and good, but it was the scoreline at the end of ninety minutes that really mattered. If he expected his players to simply serve out their time as accessories to a system then Derrida knew he wouldn't get the best out of them. He wanted them to play to their reflexes, question what was written of them, turn the expectations of failure on their head. His side might lose its shape, but at least his players would come off the pitch with heads held high, the other lot knowing they'd been in a game.

While he didn't ask his team to play to a system, neither did he just let everyone do their own thing, far from it. Barking out instructions in the mould of Sir Alex Ferguson, or lesser souls like Strachan or O'Neill, Derrida could match any of them for passion and commitment. It's just that he was honest enough to admit that neither he nor his players could be certain where it might take them. His frank admission was refreshing – though many suspected that he was writing his own dismissal notice by owning up to such a lack of faith in getting a goal. But the chairman and board of directors welcomed the chance for a dialogue with Derrida, and Jacques was one of the first to admit it was good to talk. 'Discourse anyone?' he would cheekily enquire at mealtimes, preferring to mince his words rather than tuck into *les escargots* and *pommes frites* that his chairman and directors seemed to prefer for their courses. A cheeky chappy and a bit of a 'Jacques the lad', confrontation wasn't in Derrida's vocabulary, though no one could fault him on his knowledge of extraordinarily long words. He hoped he'd get the results everyone expected of him, he'd just rather do it without a fight. Negotiating his way past defenders towards goal, he knew he couldn't simply step outside of a tradition that expected results and, being as much a part of the team as the next man, he let his feet have the last say. GOAAAL!

Index

Philosophy Football

If *Philosophical Football* tickled your footballing fancy, now prepare to adorn yourself in the colours of the most cerebrally gifted team the world has ever seen. Each of our featured players has been immortalised in a *Philosophy Football*, 100% cotton T-shirt, with their quote on the front in a nifty design, and name, plus corresponding squad number on the back. All except God. In deference to theological disputes over the authorship of the Bible, we've allocated the Number One goalie's shirt to Cain.

To add one of our number to your own personal kit-list, write or phone for a **free** catalogue.

Philosophy Football
PO Box 10684
London
N15 6XA
England

Or call us on (0181) 802 3499

Picture Credits